ANOTHER 1001 JOKES

First published in Great Britain by
Funfax Ltd., an imprint of
Dorling Kindersley Limited,
9 Henrietta Street, London, WC2E 8PS
Copyright © 2001 Funfax Ltd.
All rights reserved.

An elephant family went for a walk in the woods. "Mum, what's long, black and hairy, has six legs and is covered in red spots?" asked the young elephant. "I don't know, son," said his Mum. "Why do you ask?" "Because there's one crawling up your leg!"

Doctor, Doctor, I keep thinking I'm a rabbit.

I'm too busy to see you – hop it.

A herd of cows had formed an orchestra. What were they called? Moosicians!

What do you get if you cross a snake and a shopper? A slippery customer.

What did the young lion say? "I've joined the cubs!"

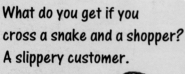

What did one sheep say to the other sheep? I want to marry ewe.

What do you get if you cross an elephant with a snowman? A jumbo yeti.

What do you get if you hang upside down from trees? A headache.

Not you again. You've been to my surgery every day for the past month.

I can't help it Doctor, I keep thinking I'm a dog.

Well, you really must stop hounding me.

What's got two legs and inspects rabbit holes? The burrow inspector.

What's yellow, has twenty-four legs and sings? Twelve canaries.

Patient: Doctor, I keep thinking I'm a pony.
Doctor: I'll give you something to make your condition more stable!

Who wrote the book, 'Coastal birds'? C. Gull.

If pigs flew planes, what would happen? Ham would go sky-high!

Keep away from that leopard.

Why?

What has six wheels and flies? A dust-cart!

He's covered in spots!

3

What's big, green and doesn't speak for hours on end? The Incredible Sulk.

What's the biggest ant in the world? A giant.

What's cowardly, wet, and full of feathers? Chicken soup.

What has two hands but no arms? A clock.

What do you call a Judge with no fingers? Justice Thumbs.

What's red and green, and sits on top of the piano going "Tick, tock, tick, tock"? A metro-gnome.

What's the best parting gift? A comb.

What's yellow and writes? A ballpoint banana.

What's brown and hops and is found in Greenland? A lost kangaroo.

What has a bottom at its top? A leg.

Why did the tap dancer retire?
He kept falling in the sink.

Why did the boy wear a belt on his teeth?
He couldn't find his braces.

What's the best way to make a pair of trousers last?
Make the coat first.

How do you send a message in the forest?
By moss code.

Who earns a living by driving their customers away?
A taxi driver.

What is white when it's dirty and black when it's clean?
A blackboard.

What did one eye say to the other?
Between you and me something smells.

Why did the scientist put a knocker on his door?
He wanted to win the no-bell prize.

Why did the man hit the clock?
Because the clock struck first.

Heard about the judge who came to a full stop?
He'd just passed sentence.

What goes oh, oh, oh?
Santa walking backwards.

A tiny volcano in Java
Appeared, but it spurted no lava.
Then a little brown mole,
With its nose through the hole,
Said: "I don't want to tunnel no farva."

A very weird fellow named Clark
Gobbled spiders up, just for a lark.
He's gone very hairy,
And looks awful scary,
But spins lovely webs in the park.

The king tossed and turned in his bed.
"I cannot get comfy," he said.
Then the queen told the king,
"You're a silly old thing!
You've still got your crown on your head."

When Timothy wanted to fly
He stood on a hilltop to try.
But he very soon found
That you can't leave the ground
Just by flapping your ears at the sky.

A bull said: "I'm Friesian. Are you?"
His friend said: "I'm very cold too.
Something warming we need
When we finish our feed.
A couple of Jerseys will do."

Ten elephants, fooling around,
Leaped into a car with a bound.
But they didn't go far
In the poor little car –
Only two metres into the ground.

A stupid young fellow called Fred
Went around with a cat on his head.
I asked "Why a cat
Do you wear as a hat?"
"Cos a horse is too heavy," he said.

A snail going jogging at dawn
Stopped to chat with a slug on the lawn.
But a thrush passing by,
With a glint in it's eye,
Gobble-gobbled, and then they
were gawn.

HELP

My barber is called Mr Bunn
He's friendly, and likes to make fun.
"A haircut?" I said,
Pointing up at my head.
"Very well," he retorted. "Which one?"

A spider grows fat and will die
If its intake of butter is high.
Much better to wait
For its web to vibrate
With a sunflower-margarine-fly.

"My glasses are lost," said Aunt Nellie.
"So tell me dear, what's on the telly?"
I told her: "There's just
Several layers of dust,
And a dead plant that's
gone rather smelly."

A young English teacher, Miss Chase,
Said her class was an utter disgrace.
"Their speech is so poor!
Take a look at the floor! –
Dropped 'H's all over
the place."

7

**Doctor, doctor, what can I do to
stop my nose running?
Put out your foot and trip it up.**

**Doctor, doctor,
everyone keeps
ignoring me.
Next, please!**

Doctor, doctor, some days
I feel like a teepee and other
days I feel like a wigwam.
You're too tense.

Doctor, doctor, I keep
thinking I'm a bridge.
What has come over you?
Lorries, buses, cars, bikes.

**Doctor, doctor,
my son swallowed a
pen, what should I do?
Use a pencil instead.**

Doctor, doctor,
I feel like a spoon.
Sit still and don't stir.

**Doctor, doctor,
can you help me out?
Of course, which way
did you come in?**

**Doctor, doctor,
I'm boiling.
Just simmer down now.**

Doctor, doctor,
everyone thinks I'm a liar.
I don't believe you.

Doctor, doctor, I can't get to sleep.
Sit on the edge of the bed and
you'll soon drop off.

OOOF!

Doctor! Doctor! I think I'm a Christmas cake.
What's got into you?
Flour, butter, mixed peel, cherries, almonds and marzipan.

Doctor, Doctor, my eyesight is failing.

Yes, it must be. This is the library.

Doctor! Doctor! I'm so tired that
I don't know where I am half the time.
Dentist: Open wide please.

Doctor! Doctor! I keep thinking I'm a carrot.
Calm down or you'll get yourself in a stew.

Doctor! Doctor! I can't stop stealing things.
Have you taken anything for it?

Doctor! Doctor! I swallowed a clock last night.
Now, don't alarm yourself.

Why did the doctor give
the ballet dancer a
bicycle pump?
Because she had
flat feet.

Doctor, doctor,
why are you writing on my toes?
Just adding a footnote.

Doctor! Doctor! Doctor! Doctor!
What on earth's the matter?
I keep seeing double.
Well sit on the sofa so
I can examine you.
Which one?

Doctor, doctor,
I feel like a pack of cards.
I'll deal with you later.

9

Why is the school football pitch always soggy?
Because the players are always dribbling.

Harry: I don't think my woodwork teacher likes me very much.
Garry: What makes you think that?
Harry: He's teaching me to make a coffin.

Mother: How do you like going to school, Sam?
Sam: Going's all right, and so is coming home.
It's the in-between that I don't like.

Teacher: Can you make a sentence with the word "fascinate" in it?
Debbie: My Dad's waistcoat has nine buttons but he can only fascinate.

Billy: What did I get for my history test?
Teacher: Well, first the good news...you spelled
your name correctly.

Teacher: You mustn't
fight, Harry. You should
learn to give and take.
Harry: I did, sir. He took
my Mars bar and I gave
him a black eye.

How are you doing at school, son?

The teacher says my marks are underwater.

What does that mean?

They're below 'C' level.

Garry: I is...
Teacher: No, Garry, You must say "I am".
Garry: All right. I am the ninth letter of the alphabet.

Sam came home from his first day at school, threw his bag on the floor and stomped upstairs, shouting, "I'm not going back tomorrow." "Why ever not, Sam?" asked his mother. "Well I can't read or write, and they won't let me talk, so what's the use?"

Teacher: Make up a sentence using the word lettuce.
Pupil: Let us out of school early.

Teacher: Simon, can you spell your name backwards?
Simon: No mis.

Teacher: When you go to the bathroom you're British, when you leave the bathroom you're British. What are you IN the bathroom?
David: European!

Teacher: Which two days of the week start with the letter 'T'?
Simon: Today and tomorrow!

Why did the teacher write the lesson on the window?
He wanted it to be very clear.

Is a hammer a good tool for maths class?
No, you need multi-pliers.

**What is the best way for a ghost-hunter to keep fit?
To exorcise regularly!**

What trees do ghosts like best? Ceme-trees.

At Ghost Academy the teacher was showing the pupils how to move right through a wall. "Now did you all follow that," said the teacher after the demonstration. "If not I'll just go through it again."

What do you call a pair of ghosts who keep pressing your doorbell? Dead ringers!

What do ghosts like to go on at a theme park? A roller ghoster!

How do you tell when a ghost is about to faint? It goes as white as a sheet!

Why did King Kong join the military academy? To study gorilla warfare!

How does a ghost count? One, BOO, Three!

What do you call a ghost who only haunts the town hall?
The night mayor.

What is a Hungarian ghost's favourite food?
Ghoul-ash!

Where do ghosts go for a haircut?
To the scaredresser.

What does a monster eat after having his teeth taken out?
The dentist!

How does Frankenstein's monster sit?
Bolt upright.

And what do ghosts eat for supper in a bell tower?
Spook-etti rings!

Where does a ghost train stop?
At a Manifestation.

A ghost in my house
by Olive N. Fear.

What do ghosts put on their roast beef?
Grave-y.

13

What is fierce, striped and lives in the garden? A tiger-lily.

What's lethal and lives underwater? The codfather.

Why do cows like being told jokes? Because they like being amoosed.

What's smoked and then hung round your neck?

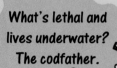

Doctor, doctor, I keep thinking I'm a goat!

When did this start?

When I was a kid!

Who wrote the book: 'Into the Lion's Den'? Hugo First.

A Kipper Tie!

What was the tortoise doing on the motorway? About one mile an hour.

Your dog chased my husband on his motorbike?

Impossible. My dog doesn't own a motorbike.

What goes woof, tick, woof tick? A watch-dog!

First snake: What's twelve minus three?
Second snake: I don't know. I'm an adder.

How do elephants dream?
They phantasize.

When is the best time to buy a canary? When it's going cheap!

What do you call a monkey that smokes?
A chimneypanzee.

What do you call a net full of fish?
A load of cods.

Why do elephants paint their toe-nails yellow?
To hide upside-down in lemon trees.

First snake:
What's your favourite game?

Second Snake:
Snakes and adders.

What's a hedgehog's favourite food?
Prickled onions!

What's orange, hairy and has two wheels?
An orang-utan on a bicycle.

What is a chimpanzee's favourite food? Gra-ape-fruit!

One morning, a man who had just moved into the neighbourhood received a parcel that, in fact, was for someone else farther down the road. So he decided to deliver it, himself. He soon arrived at the house and rang the bell.

The owner of the house was out. But this talking parrot answered,

"Who is it?"

"Your new neighbour with a parcel!" called the man, from the other side of the door.

"Who is it?" repeated the parrot.

"Your new neighbour with a parcel!" repeated the man.

"Who is it?" asked the parrot again.

"Your new neighbour with a parcel!" replied the man, becoming more and more exasperated.

"Who is it?" said the parrot, yet again. So the man answered once more.

This went on for a full hour, until the poor man became totally exhausted.

"Who is it?" said the parrot for the umpteenth time.

"Your new neighbour with a parcel!" yelled the weary man through the letterbox.

Suddenly, he collapsed with exhaustion. As he lay in the porch, the owner of the house returned and saw him.

"Who is it?" said the owner.

Just then the parrot piped up, "Your new neighbour with a parcel!"

All was quiet in the Corner Café... until the door was flung open and in came a giant monster. His five orange eyes quickly looked round the room, and he headed towards the counter, ignoring the terrified people who had taken shelter under the tables.

Unable to escape in time the café owner stood where he was behind the counter.

The shuffling, lumbering monster spoke in a voice that was surprisingly pleasant: "I'll have a glass of your best orange juice, please."

With shaking hands the café owner hastily produced a glass of orange and gave it to his strange customer.

"How much is that, please?" asked the monster.

"S-s-sixty pence," stammered the man.

With a rather impolite gurgle the monster started to drink the juice. Feeling that the monster meant to do no harm, the café owner plucked up the courage and said, "We don't often see monsters in this café."

"I'm not surprised," said the monster, "not with orange at sixty pence a glass!"

A grizzly walked up to a deer and said, "You've lost an antler!"

When the deer went to look at his own reflection in a nearby stream, he saw that his antlers were still there. The grizzly returned and told the deer that

it had lost its tail. The deer swished it and found it was still in place.

"Why do you keep on telling me things that aren't true?" the deer asked the grizzly. "I can't help it," replied the grizzly. "I'm a bear-faced liar!"

17

What has yellow and black stripes and goes Boom Boom? A bee with a bass drum!

What swims under the sea, repeating: "Who's a pretty boy then?" A parrot fish.

Where can you buy an elephant? At a jumbo-sale.

Which bird will you find underground, with a tin hat on? A Mynah bird.

What creatures live in Big Ben? The Mouses of Parliament.

What's big and ticks and swims in the river? A clockodile.

Why can't you put an elephant in the larder? It gets stuck in the door!

What is a cat's favourite dessert? Mice pudding!

Why did the elephant sit on an orange? He fancied some orange squash.

What's small and cuddly and bright purple? A koala holding its breath.

What do you call a penguin whose best friends have left him? Ice-olated.

Which animal carries an umbrella? A rain-deer.

GULP!

Which bird can be heard at mealtimes? A swallow.

What's black and white and found in Africa every summer? A penguin on holiday.

What do you call an arctic cow? An eskimoo.

What's black and white and black and white and black and white? A penguin rolling downhill.

EEK!

Why does an owl make everyone laugh? Because it's such a hoot.

What's black and shiny, and lives in a tree and is very dangerous? A crow with a machine gun.

What do you call a sleeping prehistoric animal? A dino-snore.

Waiter, have you smoked salmon?
No, madam, I've only ever smoked pipe.

How did you find your steak, sir?
Quite easily – I moved this chip aside and there it was.

Waiter, have you got soup on the menu today?
No, sir, I wiped it off.

Waiter, there's a fly in my soup.
Don't worry sir, there's a spider on the bread.

Waiter, there's a fly in my soup.
Just a moment, sir – I'll call the RSPCA.

Waiter, there's a dead fly in my soup.
Oh dear, it's the hot water that kills them.

Yuk – there's a little beetle on my salad.
Sorry, sir, I'll go and fetch you a bigger one.

Waiter, please call the manager. I can't eat this soup.
He won't want it either, sir.

I assure you our kitchens are clean sir!

Oh - is that why every thing tastes of soap!

Waiter, your thumb is in my soup.
Don't worry, sir, it's not hot.

Waiter, why is this piece of toast all broken?
Well, you said, "Toast, coffee, and step
on it," so I did.

Waiter, this lobster's only got one claw.
I'm sorry sir, it must have been in a fight.
Well, bring me the winner then.

A customer was looking at the menu in a
small restaurant. Eventually he called the
waiter over. "Waiter," he said, with a
puzzled look, "What's the difference
between your brown plate special and your
white plate special?"
"The white plate special is a pound extra, sir."
"Is the food in the white plate special
any better?"
"Not really, sir. It's just that for the white
plate special we wash the plate."

Waiter, there's a
fly playing football in
my soup!

He'll be playing in the
cup tomorrow, sir!

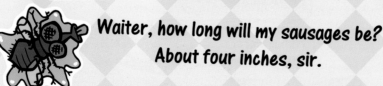

Waiter, how long will my sausages be?
About four inches, sir.

Waiter, there's a fly in my soup.
Throw him this doughnut, sir. It'll make a
good life belt.

21

Knock Knock
Who's there?
Cows go.
Cows go who?
Owls go who, cows go moo

Knock Knock
Who's there?
Hatch!
Hatch who?
That's a nasty cold you've got!

Knock Knock
Who's there?
Annie.
Annie who?
Annie thing you can do I can do better.

Knock Knock
Who's there?
Cook.
Cook who?
Stop doing bird imitations and open the door.

Knock Knock
Who's there?
Carmen.
Carmen who?
Carmen get it!

Knock Knock
Who's there?
Pudding!
Pudding who?
Pudding your shoes on before your trousers is a bad idea!

Knock knock!
Who's there?
Doctor!
Doctor who?
Yes - that's right!

Knock Knock
Who's there?
House.
House who?
House it going.

Knock Knock
Who's there?
Weed.
Weed who?
Weed better mow the lawn
before it gets too long.

Knock Knock
Who's there?
Howard.
Howard who?
Howard I know?

Knock Knock
Who's there?
Eileen.
Eileen who?
Eileen over to tie
my shoe.

Knock Knock
Who's there?
Snow.
Snow who?
Snow use, I've forgotten my
name again.

Knock Knock
Who's there?
Jamaica.
Jamaica who?
Jamaica my lunch
yet? I'm starving.

Knock Knock
Who's there?
Scott.
Scott who?
Scott nothing to do with you.

Knock Knock
Who's there?
Fred.
Fred who?
Fred this needle for
me, will you?

Knock Knock
Who's there?
Felix.
Felix who?
Felix my ice cream
again, I'll hit him.

Knock Knock
Who's there?
Luke.
Luke who?
Luke through
the keyhole
and find out.

Knock Knock
Who's there?
Ida.
Ida who?
Ida a terrible time
getting here.

23

How do you fit an elephant into a matchbox?
Take out the matches.

Why did the elephant eat a candle?
He wanted a light snack.

How do you fit a tiger into a matchbox?
Take out the elephant.

Why is a snail stronger than an elephant?
A snail carries its house – an elephant only carries its trunk.

Why is an elephant large, grey and wrinkled?
Because if it was small, white and smooth it would be an aspirin.

What is red on the outside, grey on the inside, and very crowded?
A bus full of elephants.

Why did the elephant paint his toenails red?
So he could hide in a cherry tree.

Why did the elephant paint his feet yellow?
So he could hide upside down in custard.

What time is it when an elephant sits on a fence?
Time to get a new fence.

Have you ever found an elephant in your custard?
Exactly.

Why do elephants wear green felt hats?
So they can walk across snooker tables
without being noticed.

What's grey and lights up at night?
An electric elephant.

What's big and grey and red? A sun-burnt elephant.

How do you get
down from an elephant?
You don't get down from an elephant, you get down from a duck.

How can you tell there's been an elephant in your fridge?
By the smell of peanuts and the footprints in the butter.

Do you know the
difference between
an elephant's ear
and a postbox?
No, then I'll never
send you to post a
letter again.

Why don't elephants like Penguins?
They can't get the wrapper off.

What do you get if you cross an elephant with a garden hose? A jumbo jet.

Why do elephants wear trainers? To sneak up on mice.

BOO!

What did the alien say to the books?
Take me to
your reader!

What did the cannibal say to the explorer? Nice to meat you.

What did the stamp say to the envelope? Stick with me and we'll go places.

What do you get if you cross a wolf with an egg? A very hairy omelette.

What does a bee use to brush its hair? A honeycomb.

What's the brainiest mountain in the world? Mount Cleverest.

What kind of umbrella does a Russian carry when it's raining? A wet one.

What do you call a girl who lies across a tennis court? Annette.

What travels round the world, but stays in a corner? A stamp.

What is an astronaut's favourite part of the computer? The space bar.

What do you get if you cross Dracula with a dwarf?
A vampire that gives you a nasty bite on the knee.

What do you get if you cross an encyclopedia with a pair of trousers?
Smarty Pants.

What do you get if you cross a rug and Cinderella's shoes?
Carpet slippers.

What do you get if you cross a porcupine with a mole?
Tunnels that leak.

What do you get if you cross a policeman with a tree?
A member of the special branch.

What do you get if you cross a spaniel, a poodle and a rooster?
A cockerpoodledoo.

**The Lost Hankerchief
By Ivor Snottinose**

Make Your Own Igloo
By S. K. Mo

Lion Taming for Women
By Claude R. Andoff

**Shopping by Post
By May Lauder**

**How to Feed Elephants
By P. Nutts**

How to Marry a Millionaire
By R. U. Rich

100 Quick Recipes by D. Licious

**Never Give Up
By Percy Vere**

What do spacemen play in their spare time? Astronauts and crosses.

Why did Mickey Mouse take a trip to outer space? He wanted to find Pluto.

What's the most popular sweet on Mars? Marsmallow.

How do you send a baby astronaut to sleep? Rocket.

Where do astronauts leave their cars? At parking meteors.

What do astronauts call sausages? Unidentified Frying Objects.

What did the astronaut find in his stocking at Christmas? Missile-toe.

When do astronauts eat? At launch time.

A man went to his travel agent and asked for a ticket to the Moon. "Sorry, Sir," said the assistant. "The Moon is full right now."

Which is heavier, a full moon or a half moon?
A half moon, because a full moon is lighter.

How did the alien from Jupiter count up to 32?
On its fingers.

My Dad's an astronaut. He went to a dance on Mars.
Did he stay long?
No, he said it didn't have much atmosphere.

What do you call a crazy spaceman?
An astronut.

What holds up the moon?
Moon beams.

What do men from space drink?
E-tea.

Why did the moon turn pale?
At-mos-fear.

Alien: Take me to your leader!

Take me to your leader!!!

And take your finger out of your ear when I'm talking to you.

What do you get when you cross a woodpecker with a carrier pigeon?
A bird who knocks before delivering his message.

What do you get when you cross a dog with a chicken?
A hen that lays pooched eggs.

Which bird always succeeds?
A budgie with no teeth.

Which bird grows up while it grows down?
A baby duckling.

What bird is always out of breath?
A puffin.

What do canaries eat for breakfast?
Tweetabix.

How does a chicken send a letter to her friend?
In a henvelope.

What do you get if you cross a hen with a banjo?
A chicken that plucks itself.

Where did Walt Disney get Donald Duck?
Out of a quacker.

Why do eagles sit on lecterns in churches?
Because they are birds of prey.

What do you get if you cross a parrot with a pigeon? A bird that asks the way home when it's lost.

What do you get if you cross a caged bird with a bulldog? A budgerigrrrrrrr.

Did you hear the story about the peacock? No, but I heard it's a beautiful tale.

Why do seagulls live near the sea? Because if they lived near the bay, they would be called bagels.

What bird lifts the heaviest weights? The crane.

Why did the blind chicken cross the road? To get to the birds' eye shop.

Why did the chicken walk on to the football pitch? Because the referee called for a fowl.

Why did the chicken go the séance? To get to the other side.

What do you call a witch who lives by the sea?
A sand-witch.

Why did the young witch have trouble writing letters? Because she never learned to spell properly.

How does a witch tell the time?
She looks at her witch watch.

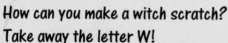

How can you make a witch scratch?
Take away the letter W!

What does a witch do if she's lost her broomstick? She has to witch-hike!

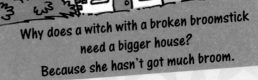

Why does a witch with a broken broomstick need a bigger house?
Because she hasn't got much broom.

Why did the witch stay at home at midnight on Hallowe'en? She couldn't stand travelling during rush hour!

Why does a witch ride on her broom?
Her vacuum cleaner's being repaired!

What would you call a motorbike belonging to a witch? A Barooooooooomstick!

What do you call a deaf witch? Anything you like, she can't hear you.

PARDON

First witch: I always buy a new hat when I'm feeling down in the dumps? Second witch: I wondered where you got them from!

What's the difference between a witch with an old broomstick and a careless witch chopping up ingredients for her magic? One's got spells in her fingers, the other's got fingers in her spells.

What goes dot-dot-dash-croak? Morse toad!

What do witches like to ride on at the theme park? The s-witchback!

Where does a witch get her pets? From a cat-alogue.

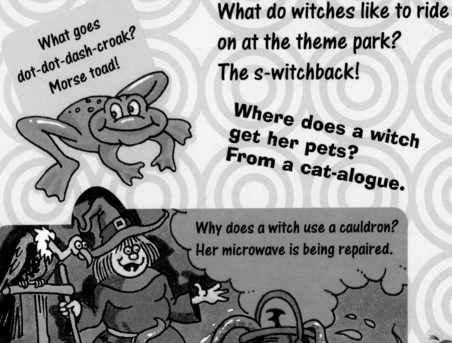

Why does a witch use a cauldron? Her microwave is being repaired.

What occurs once in every minute, twice in every moment, but never in one hundred thousand years?
The letter 'M'.

What do you call a surgeon with eight arms?
A doctopus.

Which word is always pronounced wrongly?
Wrongly.

Why is the letter 'G' scary?
It turns a host into a ghost.

What does a swimmer wear to work?
A bathing suit.

Why is it dangerous to put the letter 'M' in the refrigerator?
Because it turns ice into mice.

How do you spell 'frozen water' with three letters?
Ice.

What letter is found in cups?
'T'.

Why should we avoid the letter A?
Because it makes men mean.

Which two letters of the alphabet contain nothing?
M-T.

When is a car not a car?
When it turns into a
garage.

What's the world's
longest word?
Smiles, because there's a
mile between the first and
last letters.

What always falls
without getting hurt?
Rain.

What is full of holes yet can still
hold water?
A sponge.

What is tall, sweet and
French?
The trifle tower.

Which letters are not in the alphabet?
The ones in the letter box.

What goes ha,
ha, ha, bonk?
Someone laughing
their head off.

If Mr and Mrs Bigger had a
baby, who would be the
biggest of the three?
The baby, because he's a
little Bigger.

BURP!

What's the hardest thing
about falling out of bed?
The floor.

Who burped at the Big Bad Wolf?
Little Rude Riding Hood.

Which is the fastest,
hot or cold?
Hot – you can catch a cold.

What is Father Christmas's
wife called?
Mary Christmas.

I think we've been spotted from Venus:
A goggle eye'd monster has seen us.
It's fierce and it's red
With great horns on its head.
Three cheers for the distance between us!

A tulip bulb, down in Australia,
Exclaimed: "I'm a terrible failure!
I grew in my sleep,
But I've just had a peep,
And I think I've come up as a dahlia."

"Oh, DO hang it UP!" Mum will roar
As I drop my old coat on the floor.
So I try, but I frown,
For it always hangs DOWN
When it's put on the hook on the door.

A crab's eyes, in fair Aberdeen,
Faced backwards on stalks that were green.
It said: "While now knowing
Which way I am going,
It's good to see where I've just been."

Small children can count up to ten
On their fingers and thumbs, only when
I am counting on mine
I can reach twenty-nine
Before starting all over again!

A very keen cyclist named Eels,
Built a bike that had two oval wheels,
And if you asked why
As he passed, he'd reply:
"I just wanted to know how it feels."

There was a rude fellow called Dean,
Who swallowed a washing machine.
Now his taste buds
Are covered in suds
And all of his jokes are quite clean.

There once was a young fellow called Fred,
Who poured toffee all over his head,
So his girlfriend Ruth,
Who had a sweet tooth,
Would stick to him when they got wed.

The Owl and the Pussycat went to sea
In a beautiful pea-green boat.
But Puss was no sailor,
He came back paler,
Sporting a green fur coat.

There was a shy girl made of plastic,
Whose figure was really fantastic.
But one sunny day,
She melted away,
Still clutching her knicker elastic.

WOOF

There once was a fellow called Ollie,
Who went off to buy a Border Collie.
But in the High Street
He was swept off his feet,
And came back with a Pretty Polly.

A nervous young lady called Jane,
Was terribly sick on a train.
Folk made such a fuss,
She got on a bus,
And threw up all over again.

What do you get if you cross a centipede with a parrot?
A walkie-talkie.

What's pink and grey and has four feet?
A hippopotamus poking its tongue out.

How do you fix a chimpanzee?
With a monkey wrench.

If a dictionary goes from A to Z, what goes from Z to A?
A zebra.

What do you get if you cross a daffodil with a crocodile?
I don't know, but I wouldn't try sniffing it.

What do you get if you cross a tiger with a kangaroo?
A stripey jumper.

Why does a giraffe have such a long neck?
Because its feet smell terrible.

What did the parrot say to the spaniel?
I'm a cocker too.

What do you call a flying ape?
A hot air baboon.

What is black and white and red all over?
A sunburnt zebra.

Where does Tarzan get his loin-cloths?
From a jungle sale.

HMM, NICE.

What's black and white and very noisy?
A zebra with a drum kit.

What do you do if there's a gorilla in your bed?
Sleep in the spare room.

What goes round the jungle grunting and sending all the other animals to sleep?
A wild bore.

What card game do crocodiles like best?
Snap.

What do you call a gorilla with a machine gun?
Sir!

The mighty lion was stalking proudly through the jungle when he spotted a tiny mouse. Drawing himself up to his full height, the lion stared haughtily down at the mouse and said, "Why am I so huge and mighty, when you are so tiny, weak and insignificant?
"I've been ill" replied the mouse.

I'VE BEEN ILL!

The doctor was very good at dealing with patients who telephoned at night. His stock answer was always: "Take two aspirins and call me in the morning." One evening, however, he was very distressed to find that his loo wouldn't flush. At once he rang the plumber, who listened carefully to the doctor's description of the problem.

"Have you any aspirins, Doctor?" asked the plumber at last.

"Yes, of course."

"Well, drop two of these down the pan and if that doesn't work, call me in the morning."

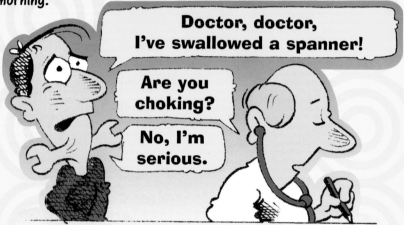

How's the little lad who swallowed the £1 coin, doctor?
No change yet, I'm afraid.

Doctor, doctor, I feel like an old sock.
Well I'll be darned.

Doctor, doctor, I feel like a symphony.
Really, I must make some notes about your case.

Doctor, doctor, I think I'm a dustbin.
Don't talk rubbish.

Jackie's mother was on the phone to the dentist. "I don't understand it," she complained. "I thought his treatment was £20, but you've charged me £80." "It is usually £20," agreed the dentist. "But Jackie yelled so loudly that three other patients ran away."

Doctor, doctor, my nose runs and my feet smell. What's wrong with me? You were made upsidedown!

Doctor, I feel like a strawberry.

You are in a jam aren't you?

Fred: Mum, I've just swallowed a spider.
Mum: Shall I get the doctor to give you something for it?
Fred: No, let it starve.

Doctor, I've developed a split personality.

Which one of you shall I see first?

Doctor: You have a bad cold. My advice is that you avoid draughts for the time being. Patient: Can I play Monopoly instead?

Doctor, I've just swallowed red, black, white, brown, yellow and blue snooker balls.

You need some greens.

Doctor, doctor, I swallowed an alarm clock last week. That could be serious – why didn't you come to see me last week? I didn't want to alarm anybody.

How does Wolf Man travel when he's got fleas? By itch-hiking.

Why did the witch go to the psychiatrist? Because she thought everyone loved her.

What do you call a witch with one leg? Eileen.

What do you call a monster Scotsman? Mac-abre.

What did the young witch say to her mother? Can I have the keys to the broom tonight?

Why won't a witch wear a flat cap? Because there's no point in it.

How do witches drink tea? With cups and sorcerors.

Doctor: Do stop sucking your thumb. Take it out of your mouth... I'll sew it back on in a minute!

What do you call a witch who lives by the sea and wouldn't say boo to a ghost? A chicken sand-witch.

What's the best thing for water on the brain?

A tap on the head.

What do you get if you cross a witch and an ice cube? A cold spell.

What do you call two witches that share a room? Broom mates.

First witch: I have the face of a sixteen-year-old girl.
Second witch: I think you'd better give it back – you're getting it all wrinkled.

How is the witches team doing? They're having a spell in the first division.

Have you heard about the good weather witch? She's forecasting sunny spells.

What goes cackle, cackle, squelch, squelch? A witch in soggy trainers.

Why don't ghosts wearing
trousers use pocket calculators?
They already know how many pockets they've got!

Did you hear about the stupid ghost?
He kept climbing over walls!

What walks backwards through
walls going, "Oh, er, boo"?
A nervous ghost.

What's a skeleton's favourite instrument? A trom-bone.

What do ghosts
call their navy?
The Ghost Guard.

What is a ghost's favourite stage musical?
The Human of the Opera.

What do
short-sighted
ghosts wear?
Spooktacles.

What do ghosts like
to play at parties?
Haunt and seek.

Why don't skeletons play music in church? They have no organs.

44

What do you flatten a ghost with?
A spirit level.

First Ghost: I keep bumping into things.

Second Ghost: Have you had your eyes checked?

First Ghost: No, they've always been this colour.

What is a ghost boxer called?
A phantomweight.

Which ghost ate too much porridge?
Ghouldilocks.

**Looking at Ghosts
By I. C. Throughyou**

The Haunted House
By Hugo First

How did the glamorous ghoul earn a living?
She was a cover ghoul.

Why didn't the ghost jump off the cliff?
He didn't have the guts to do it.

Do you ever have problems making up your mind?

Well...er, yes and no.

Why was Dracula's young son a disgrace to the family?
He couldn't stand the sight of blood.

What is a vampire's second favourite fruit?
Neck-tarines.

What is a vampire's favourite dance?
The fang-dango!

Why is Hollywood full of vampires?
They need someone to play the bit parts.

What does a vampire doctor call out to his patients in the waiting room?
Neckst!

What comes out at night and goes: flap, flap, chomp, chomp, yikes!?
A vampire with toothache.

What does a vampire with only one fang do?
Grin and bare it.

What do you get if you cross Dracula with a snail?
The world's slowest vampire.

Who was Dracula's favourite hero?
Captain Blood.

Why was Dracula a good artist? Because he could draw blood.

Vampire Fighting By Ivor Cross

First Vampire: Last night I bit into a bar of soap by mistake!
Second Vampire: Were you angry?
First Vampire: Angry? I was foaming at the mouth.

What kind of mail does a superstar vampire get? Fang-mail.

Why do vampires make bad football keepers? Because they can't handle crosses.

Which is Dracula's favourite ice cream flavour? Veinilla.

Will Dracula write his memoirs? He's no time for reflections!

A family of four elephants was going on holiday. When the taxi arrived to take them to the airport, the taxi-driver was puzzled. "How will I get you all in my car?" he asked.
"Easy," said one elephant. "Two in the front seat, two in the back, and our trunks in the boot."

What key won't fit in a lock? A monkey.

What's pink, fat, and waves a wand? A fairy elephant.

A bee opened a theatre and was wondering whether or not to put on a Shakespeare play first. What did he say? "To bee or not to bee".

Why do elephants wear sunglasses? So no one recognizes them in a crowd.

What's dangerous and shoots out of trees? A squirrel with a pea-shooter.

Which animals were the last to leave the ark? The elephants – they were packing their trunks.

Why was the cockerel upset? Because he was feeling hen-pecked.

A horse decided to go into town. He saw a posh hotel and wanted to stay there.
"Have you a room for me please?" he asked the receptionist.
The receptionist could hardly believe his eyes. "I don't think I would have one that's suitable for a horse!" he said.
"Of course you have" said the horse. "Give me the bridle suite."

What do you call an elephant who keeps watching TV?
A telly-phant.

Three pigs standing together:
First Pig: I'd stay away from him!
Second Pig: Why?
First Pig: Because he's a boar!

What's grey and goes round in circles?
An elephant in a tumble-drier.

What do you call a cat that's accident-prone?
A cat-astrophe.

What do you call an elephant that's taken a mud bath?
A smelly-phant.

Which animal should you never play games with?
A cheetah.

Doctor, I'm frightened I'll be snatched by a giant eagle.

You mustn't get carried away.

49

Did you know that eight out of ten schoolchildren use ballpoint pens to write with?
Gosh! What do the other two use them for?

Why did the flea fail his exam?
He wasn't up to scratch.

Why did the hockey teacher give her team torches?
Because they kept losing their matches.

Why did the schoolboy take the mop to the soccer lesson on Mondays?
Because that's the day they practised dribbling.

Dinner lady: Eat your greens: they're good for growing children.
Joe: Who wants to grow children?

Why is school like a shower?
One wrong turn and you're in hot water.

What's the longest piece of furniture in the school?
The multiplication table.

Librarian: Johnnie, be quiet. The juniors can't read.
Johnnie: Hm! I could when I was their age.

Why did the boy take a hammer to school at the end of term?
It was breaking up day.

MEOW!

Teacher: Give me a sentence with the words "defence", "defeat" and "detail" in it.
Pupil: When the horse jumps over defence, defeat go before detail.

Why was the headmaster worried?
Because there were too many rulers in school.

Why did the jelly bean go to school?
He wanted to be a smarty.

Polly: I think my teacher loves me.
Sam: Why?
Polly: She keeps putting "x"s next to my work.

Teacher: What do you know about the Dead Sea?
Pupil: I didn't even know it was ill.

"Now, children," said the headmistress as the school party prepared to board the Channel ferry, "What do you shout if one of the boys falls into the sea?"
Up went Sam's hand. "Boy overboard!" he said.
"Good boy – now what do you shout if one of the teachers falls into the sea?"
"Depends which teacher it is."

Teacher: I wish you'd pay a little more attention.

Pupil: I'm paying as little as I can!

51

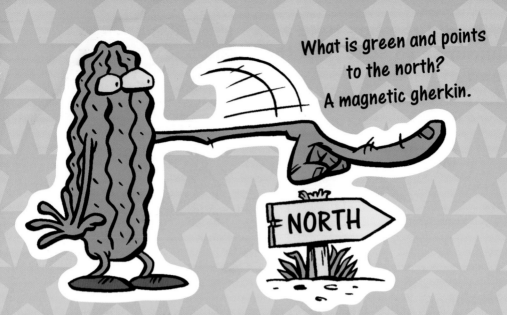

What is green and points to the north?
A magnetic gherkin.

What's green, hairy and takes tablets?
A gooseberry with a headache.

What's worse than finding a maggot in your apple?
Finding half a maggot in your apple.

What's yellow and goes "Splutter, splutter, splutter!"?
A lemon running out of juice.

What's red and green and wears boxing gloves?
A fruit punch.

What's yellow and always points North?
A magnetic banana.

What did the elephant say to the lemon?
Let's play squash.

What's purple and sits in a bowl of custard shouting "Help!"?
A damson in distress.

What is purple and hums?
An electric plum.

What sits in the custard
looking cross?
Apple grumble.

Why are bananas
never lonely?
Because they hang
around in bunches.

What do you give an
injured lemon?
Lemonade.

What's green and hairy and
wears sunglasses?
A gooseberry on holiday.

What do you do with a blue banana?
Try to cheer it up.

COME ON –
CHEER UP!

What's green and
ruled Russia?
Catherine the Grape.

What comes out of
the ground at ninety
miles an hour?
A turbo-charged
carrot.

What's green on the
outside and yellow on
the inside?
A banana disguised
as a cucumber.

How do you make an apple
turnover?
Push it down hill.

UH!

The raindrops make
things beautiful,
The grass and
flowers too.
If rain can make
things beautiful,
Why doesn't it
rain on you?

Piggy on the railway, picking up stones.
Along came a train and broke
poor Piggy's bones.
"Hey," said Piggy, "that's not fair!"
"Tough," said the driver,
"I don't care."

Mary had a little lamb,
You've heard it all before.
But then she asked
for seconds,
And had a little more.

My girlfriend in the mountains
Is very shy and meek.
She always dresses in the dark
In case the mountains peek.

Little Jack Horner
Sat in his corner
Eating his cold meat pie.
He caught salmonella,
Unfortunate fella,
And now is likely to die.

There's a peanut sitting on the railway track,
His heart is all a-flutter.
The train comes roaring round the bend –
Toot! Toot! – peanut butter.

Little Miss Muffet
Sat on a tuffet
Eating her Irish stew.
Along came a spider
And sat down beside her,
So Miss Muffet ate him too.

54

A lady from Kalamazoo
Gave her pets a
hot vindaloo.
Now the cat is dead –
It exploded when fed
And the dog can't stay out of
the loo.

There was a young soldier from France,
Who asked a young hippie to dance.
But whilst doing the cancan,
His glass eye fell out, man,
And shattered all hopes of romance.

A cat burglar called Nick O'Shea,
Realised that crime doesn't pay.
When an ugly old bat
With her hair in a plait,
Begged him to take HER away.

There was a young fellow named Pete,
Who ate ninety-two shredded wheat.
Now his arms are much stronger,
And twenty feet longer,
From gripping the toilet seat.

There once was a young lady called Nellie,
Who dropped some ice cream on her belly.
It being just a trifle
Her screams she did stifle,
But both her legs turned into jelly.

Which fish wears a cowboy hat and two guns?

Billy the Squid.

What do thieves eat for dinner? Beefburglars.

Stan: The police are looking for a man with a hearing aid. Dan: Why aren't they using glasses?

Why do robbers wear braces? Because they're hold up men!

Who never minds being interrupted in the middle of a sentence?

A convict.

"I'll have to report you," said the traffic cop to the driver. "You were doing 85 miles per hour." 'Rubbish, officer!" replied the driver, "I've only been in the car for ten minutes."

Why hasn't anyone ever stolen a canal? It has too many locks.

What do you call a person who breaks into a shop and steals all the bacon? A hamburglar.

Newsreader: The artist who has been forging Picassos has been sent to prison. Naturally he says he was framed.

Policeman: Sorry, son, you'll need a permit to fish here.
Harry: No thanks, I'm doing pretty well with a worm.

A policeman saw a little girl walking along the street dragging an old scrubbing brush on a piece of string and saying, "Walkies!".
"Nice dog you've got there, kid," said the kindly policeman, stopping to pat the brush.
The little girl gave him a look of purest scorn.
"That isn't a dog!" she said. "It's an old scrubbing brush!"
"Sorry," said the embarrassed policeman, and walked on.
As soon as he had gone the little girl bent down and stroked the brush. "That fooled him, didn't it, Fido!" she said.

Newsreader: Two prisoners have escaped from jail. One is seven feet tall and the other is four foot nine. Police are looking high and low for them.

Two convicts were sewing mailbags in prison.
"I shouldn't be here," said one.
"I committed the perfect bank robbery, got £100,000, and then I made my big mistake."
"What did you do wrong?"
"I stayed to count the money."

**Dolly: If I dug a hole in the middle of the park, what would come up?
Polly: Probably a policeman.**

Which animal has the highest intelligence?
A giraffe.

Which dog wears contact lenses?
A cock-eyed spaniel.

Why did the ape put a hamburger on his head?
He thought he was a griller.

Why did the spider like computers?
Because he had his own web site.

Why should you never attack an octopus?
Because it's very well armed.

What do you call a deer with no eyes?
No idea.

And what do you call a deer with no eyes and no legs?
Still no idea.

How do hens dance?
Chick to chick.

What do you call a dog in jeans and a sweater?
A plain clothes police dog.

Why did a parrot and an owl keep quarrelling? Because the parrot called the owl a twit and the owl kept replying "Twit-to-you!"

What do you get if you cross a hedgehog with a giraffe? A long necked toothbrush!

What do a potato and a spider have in common? Neither of them can fly a plane!

Did you hear about the thief who took half a pound of almonds, half a pound of brazils and a bag of peanuts? Sounds like a nut to me.

Why are skunks always arguing? Because they like to raise a stink.

What goes red, yellow, green, yellow, red? A packet of fruit sweets.

An elephant walked into a baker's and asked for a dozen buns. The assistant froze on the spot and just stared unable to speak.
"What's the matter with her?" the elephant asked a second white-faced assistant.
"W...we don't see elephants in here, v...very often!" quavered the girl, nervously.
"I'm not surprised," snapped the elephant, "when you're such a long way from the bus stop!"

What is a queue-jumper? A kangaroo on a billiard table.

What do you call a man with a car on his head?
Jack.

What's orange and comes rushing out of the ground at 150kph?
An E-type carrot.

Which type of snake sits on car windscreens?
Windscreen vipers.

Why is a baby like an old car?
Because they both rattle.

Two wizards in a car were driving along and the police were chasing them for speeding. One said, "What are we going to do?" The other replied, "Quick, turn the car into a side street."

Why can't cars play rugby?
Because they've only got one boot.

When is a car not a car?
When it turns into a garage.

Which part of a car is the laziest?
The wheels, because they are always tyred.

Which type of car does a lady in a pantomime drive?
A Dame-ler.

What do drivers of old bangers want more than anything else?
A speeding ticket.

What's the difference between an old banger and a school?
A school breaks up, and an old banger breaks down.

What would you have if your car's motor caught fire?
A fire engine.

"This car has had one careful owner, sir," said the salesman.
"But it's covered with dents and scratches!"
"I'm afraid the other owners weren't so careful."

Fred: What sort of car has your Dad got?
Ken: I can't remember the name, but I know it starts with T.
Fred: Ours starts with gas.

What do you call an old banger with a sunroof?
A skip.

What do you call a suped-up old banger?
A lawnmower.

Was Dracula ever married?
No, he was a bat-chelor!

Don't go near Dracula by Al Scream

How does Dracula like to have his food served?
In bite-size pieces.

Did you hear about the vampires who went mad?
They went completely batty.

Who did the vampire marry?
The girl necks door.

Which boats do vampires like?
Blood vessels.

Can a toothless vampire bite you?
No, but he can give you a nasty suck.

What does Dracula say when you tell him a new fact?
Well, fangcy that!

What is Dracula's favourite pudding?
Leeches and scream.

Why is Dracula such a nuisance?
Because he's a pain in the neck.

Which is Dracula's favourite animal? A giraffe..think of all that neck.

What's a vampire's favourite dance? The vaults.

First Vampire: A tramp stopped me in the street and told me he hadn't had a bite for days.
Second Vampire: What did you do?
First Vampire: I bit him.

Did you hear about the vampire who died of a broken heart? He loved in vein.

Why might vampires be taken in easily? Because they're known to be suckers.

What's Dracula's favourite Star Wars movie? The Vampire Strikes Back.

What did the vampire say to his girlfriend? "After the film, do you fancy a quick bite?"

What's a duck's favourite food? Cream quackers.

What did the sick chicken say? "I have the people pox."

Joe: There are two ducks over there. Which one do you want?
Ian: Eider!

What do duck decorators do? Paper over the quacks.

What's the favourite food of geese? Gooseberries.

Which birds spend all their time on their knees? Birds of prey.

Why is a sofa like a roast chicken? Because they're both full of stuffing.

What do you get if you cross a flame and a duck? A firequacker.

What do lovesick owls say to each other when it's raining?
"Too-wet-to-woo."

What cry do Scottish owls make?
Hoots mon.

What's an owl's favourite book?
Whooo's Whoooo.

What does an educated owl say?
"Whom".

What sits in the trees going "Tooh, Tooh!"?
A backward owl.

What do you get if you cross an owl with a goat?
A hootenanny.

How do you know that owls are cleverer than chickens?
Have you ever heard of the Kentucky fried owl?

Why are owls such good comedians?
Because they keep their audiences in hoots of laughter.

What's a cleaner's favourite fairy tale? Sweeping Beauty.

Why did Mickey Mouse want to have a flight on the space shuttle? Because he wanted to find Pluto.

Which part did the milkmaid get in Cinderella? The dairy godmother.

Why was Cinderella thrown out of the rugby team? Because she kept running away from the ball.

Why was there always music in Sherwood Forest? Because Robin had a band of Merry Men.

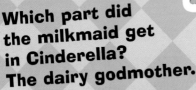

How did Robin Hood tie his shoelaces? With a long bow.

What's wrapped in clingfilm and hangs around French cathedrals? The lunchpack of Notre Dame.

Where did the Merry Men go to buy their sweets? The Friar Tuck shop.

Which cartoon character has antlers and wears white gloves? Mickey Moose.

Why did Robin Hood lose the archery contest?
Because his arrows were all a quiver.

What's a traffic warden's favourite Disney film? Aladdin and the Magic Clamp.

Why did Aladdin's palace have no bathrooms in it?
Because he was filthy rich.

What were the outlaws' favourite birds? Crows and sparrows.

Why did Puss in Boots suck lemons?
Because he was a sourpuss.

Which fairy tale character enjoys parties the most? Rapunzel – she always lets her hair down.

Why did Goldilocks stir the porridge so hard?
Because Daddy Bear told her to beat it.

Joe: Which fairy tale character should you never tell a secret to?
Ann: I don't know.
Joe: Jack.
Ann: Why?
Joe: Because Jack and the Beanstalk.

What was the outlaws' favourite musical instrument? The loot.

Why did Hansel and Gretel cry after they ate the witch's gingerbread house?
Because they had lumps in their throats.

What did Tom Thumb drink every day? Condensed milk.

How did the heartbroken frog die?
It kermitted suicide.

What do you get if you cross a frog with a ferry?
A hopper craft.

Where do frogs leave their hats?
In the croakroom.

Did you hear about the frog that parked on a double yellow line?
It got toad away.

Where do frogs sit?
On toadstools.

What do you get if you cross frogs and iguanas?
Leaping lizards.

How does a frog feel when he has a broken leg?
Unhoppy.

What's white on the outside, green on the inside, and comes with relish and onions?
A hot frog.

Which frog spied for its country?
James Pond.

What's a frog spy known as?

A croak and dagger agent.

What's green and goes dah-dit, dah-dah, dah-dit?
Morse toad.

What goes Croak! Croak! when it's misty?
A froghorn.

What's a frog's favourite sweet?
Lollihops.

What's green and turns red at the flick of a switch?
A frog in a liquidizer.

What kind of shoes do frogs like?
Open toad sandals.

Where do frogs keep their money?
In a river bank.

What do stylish frogs wear?
Jumpsuits.

What do frogs do with paper?
Rip it.

What's brown on the outside, green on the inside and hops?
A frog sandwich.

"Who's been eating my porridge?" asked Daddy Bear.

"Nevermind the porridge, where's the video?" said Baby Bear.

What do you call a bald teddy? Fred bear.

A jolly old bear at the Zoo
Could always find something to do.
When it bored him to go
On a walk to and fro
He reversed, and walked fro and to.

A family of polar bears were sitting on an iceberg. Mother Bear said, "I have a tale to tell." So she told the story of how the bear got his fur coat.

"I have a tale to tell too," said Father Bear. And he recounted the story of how the bear got his sharp teeth.

Baby Bear shifted uncomfortably on the chilly iceberg.

"My tail's told!" he complained.

Which bear is white and smells of peppermint? A polo bear.

Which bear needs a deoderant? Pooh Bear.

Fred: So I grabbed my gun and shot the bear in my pyjamas.

Sally: How wonderful! But why was the bear wearing your pyjamas?

What goes dot-dot-dash-dash-squeak?
Mouse code.

Which rodents are the most athletic?
Track and field mice.

What do you call four singing female rodents?
The Mice Girls.

What do you get if you cross rabbits with termites?
Bugs bunnies.

What's grey and squirts jam at you?
A mouse eating a doughnut.

What's the best way to catch rabbits?
Hide in the woods and make a noise like a lettuce.

What do you get if you cross a cow with a rabbit?
A hare in your milk.

What pet always has a big smile?
A grinny pig.

What's the definition of a row of rabbits stepping backwards?
A receding hare line.

How do rabbits keep their hair in place?
With hare spray.

What do ghosts take
for bad colds?
Coffin drops.

**What do
vampires
learn at
school?
The alpha-bat!**

What sort of song
does a ghost sing?
A haunting melody.

**How does a girl vampire
flirt with a boy vampire?
By batting her eyelids.**

Why don't bats live alone?
They like to hang around with their friends.

**What do witches
wear on their hair?
Scare spray.**

**How did the skeleton
know it was going to
rain?
He could feel it in
his bones.**

A snail was returning home
late one night and had to cut
through a dark alleyway.
As he was going down it, he
was mugged by two slugs. At
the police station, a policeman
asked him, "Can you give me
a description of your
attackers?" The snail
pondered this for a moment,
and then replied, "I'm not
sure...it all happened
so quickly."

"You don't look very well, Wolfman," said a monster friend. "In fact, you look as if you're going to the dogs!"

What does a monster do if he loses his hand? He goes to a second-hand shop.

Why do pixies have such bad table manners? Because they're always goblin.

What's a monster's favourite James Bond film? 'Ghoulfinger'.

What do you call a blood sucking creature that crashes into a fruit tree? A jam-pire.

What does the Abominable Snowman say when he doesn't think something is possible? Snow way.

What do you give to the Elephant Man if he needs calming down? A trunkquilizer.

Why does Frankenstein walk so stiffly? Because the laundry put too much starch in his underpants!

What do you call a monster in a witch's cauldron?
Stu.

What do you call a ghost doctor?
A surgical spirit.

What do you call a giant, ten-armed, wild-eyed monster that has you cornered in a room?
Sir!

What do you call someone who puts across ghosts' points of view?
A spooksperson!

What do you call people who try to thumb a lift at midnight?
Witch-hikers.

How did the monster cure his sore throat?
He spent all day gargoyling.

What's a vampire's son called?
Bat Boy.

Why did the monster stop playing with his brother?
He got tired of kicking him around.

74

Who says 'Shiver me Timbers'
on a ghost ship?
The skeleton crew.

**Why did the
skeleton go to
the party?
For a rattling
good time.**

**Which type of
monster can sit at
the end of your
finger?
The bogey man.**

**Who won the Monster
Beauty Competition?
No-one.**

Who can you always trust with a secret?
A mummy...they always keep things
under wraps.

**Did you hear about the
unlucky princess?
She kissed a handsome prince
and he turned into a toad.**

**What did one
Invisible Man say
to the other?
Nice not to see
you again.**

Why do ghosts never take their children out at night
when it's raining?
It dampens their spirits.

Who has green hair and runs through the forest?
Mouldy locks.

Why did the computer sneeze?
It had a virus.

If all your clothes were stolen, what would you go home in?
The dark.

Where do computers like to dance?
At a disk-o.

Why would Snow White make a great judge?
Because she's the fairest of them all.

Which type of flower grows between your nose and your chin?
Tulips.

What do computers do when they get hungry?
They eat chips.

What is the centre of gravity?
The letter 'v'.

What does a caterpillar do on New Year's Day?
Turn over a new leaf.

What did one stick insect say to another?
Stick around.

What is the definition of a narrow squeak?
A thin mouse.

Which star is dangerous?
A shooting star.

Which two things can't you have for breakfast?
Lunch and dinner.

What time do you go to the dentist?
Tooth-hurty.

Why is it not safe to doze on trains?
Because they run over sleepers.

What's at the end of everything?
The letter 'G'.

What gets wetter the more it dries?
A towel.

Why isn't your nose 12 inches long?
Because then it would be a foot.

Which months have 28 days?
All of them.

Which are the two words with the most letters?
Post Office.

There are three kinds of people in the world – those who can count, and those who can't.

How do footballers stay cool?
They sit next to the fans.

Who wrote the book, 'Flying over the Ocean'? Albert Ross.

What dance does an eel do? The conger.

Which bird never stops eating? A gannet.

First elephant: Think of six things with milk in them.
Second elephant: A milkshake, custard, ice-cream and three cows.

Which kind of bee drops things? A fumble bee.

Who wrote the book, 'Life of a Fool'? Irma Jackass.

George: That electric eel is a bright spark.
Ellie: Yes, he likes to keep up with current events.

Why did the crab play the violin? Because he was a fiddler.

First horse:
Will you make the after-dinner speech toinght?

Second horse:
Why can't you?

First horse:
Because I'm shire.

What's small, green and highly explosive?
A frog with a stick of dynamite.

What is a sheep's favourite sweet?
A chocolate baa.

If a pig were crossed with the Tower of Pisa, what would you end up with?
Lean bacon.

Who wrote the book, 'Prehistoric Birds'?
Terry Dactyl.

What do you get if you cross an Egyptian hat and a top model?

Not just a pretty fez!

Which bird always jeers at you?
A mockingbird.

If an elephant goes for a run and ends up out of breath, what do you call him?
An elepant.

What hops about down under
and buzzes?
A wallabee!

What do you get if you cross
a kangaroo with a hippo?
A hopopotamus.

A skunk was sleeping by the river, with his tail hanging in the water. Suddenly, a huge fish came up and seized the skunk by his tail. "I've caught him," thought the fish, "hook, line and stinker!"

How does a fox keep his home clean?

With his brush.

First Seal:
Can you keep a
secret?

Second Seal:
Of course, my lips
are sealed.

Which bird is
always playing
around?
A lark.

Knock, Knock,
Who's there?
Gibbon.
Gibbon who?
Gibbon the chance
I'd like to come in.

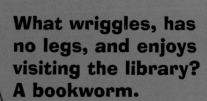

What wriggles, has
no legs, and enjoys
visiting the library?
A bookworm.

Billy: I'm stuck on my homework. Your Mum's very clever, does she know where the arctic fox comes from? Sally: Of course. Alaska!

What do cows cut the lawn with? A mooer.

When do chimpanzees itch and eat? At the chimps' flea party.

What do you get if you cross a French Emperor and a crab? Nipoleon.

What did the slug say as he slipped down the window very quickly? How slime flies.

Why couldn't the dog bark? Because he was a bit husky.

What's the definition of a polygon? An empty parrot cage.

What do you call a baby donkey? An asset!

81

What happens to you if you eat Christmas decorations?
You get tinselitis.

Why did Santa crash into the house? Because the children left the landing lights on.

Who delivers Christmas presents to the police?
Santa Clues.

What do you call a canary that flies into the Christmas pudding?
Tweetie Pie.

Which Russian king visited Jesus in the manger?
The Tsar of Bethlehem.

Who cooks Christmas dinner in the monastery?
The head friar.

What do you get if you cross a turkey with a dumb owl?
A festive bird that doesn't give a hoot for Christmas.

Aunty: For our next Christmas dinner I'm going to cross a turkey with an octopus.
Rakeem: What on earth for?
Aunty: So we can all have a leg each.

What happens to you at Christmas?
Yule be happy.

When do sailors put to sea at Christmas?
At yule-tide.

Mum: Why haven't I heard you saying your prayers?
Jonny: Because I wasn't talking to you.

What did the vicar say when his church caught fire?
Holy Smoke!

Why did the vicar walk on his hands?
Because he thought it was Palm Sunday.

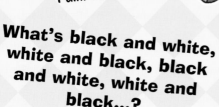

Who won the Church Beauty Competition?
One of the church belles.

What's black and white, white and black, black and white, white and black...?
A nun who's just been pushed down a hill.

Tourist: How many church bells are there in this town?
Guide: About twenty, all tolled!

What's black and white and roars with laughter?
The nun who pushed her.

What's the difference between a church bell and a pickpocket?
One peals from the steeple, the other steals from the people.

Where would you look for a lost vicar?
At the Missing Parsons Bureau.

A six-year-old girl named Grace,
Complained of a lump on her face.
Said her mum, "I suppose
It could be your nose,
It seems to be in the right place."

When a man named Michael O'Shea,
First drove on the motorway,
A big notice in red
Said, "Clean Toilets Ahead",
So he cleaned half a dozen that day.

A bachelor laddie from Fife,
Was searching around for a wife.
He found quite a few,
But he's settled
for two.
Now he's leading a
double life.

A fellow residing in Staines,
Was not over-blessed with brains.
He gave his umbrella
To some other fella,
Now he can't venture out when it rains.

The ugliest girl in Bude
Went swimming one day in the nude.
There were fish by the score
That swam to the shore,
Where they stood on the beach and booed.

There was a young man from Troon,
With a head like a hot-air balloon.
He took off his socks
Which were weighted with rocks,
And he floated away to the moon.

An unfortunate flea named Sid,
Got trapped in a teapot – he did.
Though he swam up the spout,
He couldn't get out
Until someone took off the lid.

There is a poor girl named Theresa,
Who's got herself locked in the freezer.
She doesn't look nice
Encased in ice,
So let's hope that nobody sees her.

A man in a pub said, "I think
There's a black hairy thing in my drink."
Said the barmaid, quite cool,
"It's a false eyelash, you fool!
It sometimes falls off when I blink."

There was a small boy named Ben,
Who said he could count up to ten.
But he only reached six
When he got in a fix,
And had to start over again.

There was a young fellow from Kent,
Whose nose was gigantic, and bent.
He could – so we hear,
Sniff in his ear,
But that was as far as it went.

What's the difference between an angry audience and a cow with a sore throat?
One boos madly and the other moos badly.

What did the arthritis say to the rheumatism?
"Let's get out of this joint."

What did one raindrop say to another raindrop?
"Two's company; three's a cloud."

What's the difference between a fidget and someone who's bankrupt?
One can't settle down, the other can't settle up.

What did the necklace say to the crown?
"You go on ahead; I'll hang around for a while."

What's the difference between a newspaper and a TV set?
Ever tried swatting a fly with a TV set?

What's the difference between the North Pole and the South Pole?
That's a question of degrees.

What did Charles 1 say just before he was executed?
"Can I go for a walk around the block?"

What did the wall say to the plug?
"Socket to me, baby."

What did the chocolate say to the lollipop?
"Hello, sucker."

What's the difference between a composer and a postman?
One writes notes, the other delivers them.

What did the jack say to the car?
"Want a lift?"

Dan: I say, I say, I say! Did you hear the joke about the bed that needed changing?

Stan: No, tell me.

Dan: I can't. It hasn't been made yet.

How do you get rid of varnish? Take away the letter R.

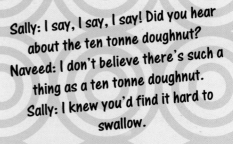

Mark: I say, I say, I say! Did you hear the joke about the cornflake?

Gary: No, tell me.

Mark: I'll tell you the first part now and the second part this afternoon.

Gary: Why can't you tell me it all at once?

Mark: Because it's a cereal.

What do you call a woman who doesn't like butter? Marge.

Why did the apple turnover? Because it saw the jam roll.

Sally: I say, I say, I say! Did you hear about the ten tonne doughnut?

Naveed: I don't believe there's such a thing as a ten tonne doughnut.

Sally: I knew you'd find it hard to swallow.

Which fruit grew on Noah's Ark? Pears.

Lilly: I say, I say, I say! My dog plays chess.

Billy: He must be a very clever dog.

Lilly: Not really...he's only beaten me twice.

What did the cookie say to the half-eaten biscuit? "Oh, crumbs."

Knock! Knock!
Who's there?
Juan.
Juan who?
Juan of those things sent to annoy you.

Knock! Knock!
Who's there?
Colin.
Colin who?
Colin and see me next time you're passing.

Knock! Knock!
Who's there?
Yvonne.
Yvonne who?
Yvonne to know how many people live here.

Knock! Knock!
Who's there?
Sarah.
Sarah who?
Sarah doctor in the house.

Knock! Knock!
Who's there?
Distress.
Distress who?
Distress hardly covers my knees.

Knock! Knock!
Who's there?
Ivor.
Ivor who?
Ivor awful headache. Any tablets?

Knock! Knock!
Who's there?
Duncan.
Duncan who?
Duncan make your garden grow.

Knock! Knock!
Who's there?
Leaf.
Leaf who?
Leaf me alone!

Knock! Knock!
Who's there?
Cereal.
Cereal who?
Cereal pleasure to meet you.

Knock! Knock!
Who's there?
Ben.
Ben who?
Ben Doon and lick my boots.

Knock! Knock!
Who's there?
Ben.
Ben who?
Ben knocking on your door all afternoon.

Knock! Knock!
Who's there?
Accordion.
Accordion who?
Accordion to the forecast, it's going to rain tomorrow.

Knock! Knock!
Who's there?
Aladdin.
Aladdin who?
Aladdin the street is waiting for you.

Knock! Knock!
Who's there?
Woody.
Woody who?
Woody you want?

Knock! Knock!
Who's there?
Closure.
Closure who?
Closure mouth when you're eating.

Knock! Knock!
Who's there?
Irish.
Irish who?
Irish I had a million pounds.

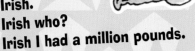

Knock! Knock!
Who's there?
Godfrey.
Godfrey who?
Godfrey tickets for the football match.

Knock! Knock!
Who's there?
Ice cream soda.
Ice cream soda who?
Ice cream soda neighbours wake up.

Knock! Knock!
Who's there?
Icy.
Icy who?
Icy your underwear.

Knock! Knock!
Who's there?
Despair.
Despair who?
Despair tyre is flat.

Knock! Knock!
Who's there?
MP.
MP who?
My glass is MP. Can you get me some water?

89

There was a young man from Seattle,
Whose big end developed a rattle.
Said the doctor, "Don't panic!
Get a motor mechanic.
I'm fighting a losing battle."

There was a young girl from Penzance,
Who said she had ants in her pants.
She writhed, and she wriggled,
While spectators giggled,
And thought she was doing a dance.

As scientists aim for the stars,
I'm certain there's life on Mars.
Those little green men
Gave the game away when
They exported their chocolate bars.

There was a strange fellow from Crewe,
Who got himself into a stew.
The carrots and meat
Got under his feet,
And the dumplings obscured his view.

A young lady travelling to Leicester,
Indulged in a little siesta.
But so risky they are
In a fast moving car,
That a traffic cop had to arrest her.

A turkey dreads the end of November,
Because it is forced to remember,
That it's ultimate fate,
Is stuffed, roast, on a plate,
Very soon – 25th December.

The hundred and second dalmation,
Was stranded alone at the station,
For the hundred and one,
Had already gone,
Leaving him in a dire situation.

Santa Claus said, "I'm sorry to say,
I have ruined my own Christmas Day,
It's not very pleasant!
I don't have a present!
It must have been given away."

An unpunctual woman named Kate,
Though she ran, was always hours late,
She arrived at each place,
Out of breath, red of face,
In a sweaty and untidy state.

A queasy and seasick old Viking,
Said, "It really is **NOT** to my liking,
To be always afloat,
In this leaky old boat,
I'd rather we travelled by cycling."

What do you call a monster with rabbits in his ears? Warren.

Why does a red-breasted bird always fly after Count Dracula?

Because you always find Robin with Batman.

Why aren't vampires very good at telling lies? They can't cross their fingers.

Which puzzles do vampires not like? Crosswords!

Which kind of animals do vampires keep? Bat-tery hens.

How do you break down the door to Dracula's castle? Use a bat-tering ram!

Which is a ghost's favourite food? I scream and boo-berry pie.

How do vampires like their fish served? In a bat-ter.

Where does the Abominable Snowman go for a dance?
To a snowball.

Why did the monster boy swallow a 50p piece?
It was his dinner money.

Did you hear about the mad scientist who invented an acid so strong that it can burn through anything? He's now trying to invent something to keep it in.

Why was Frankenstein never lonely?
Because he was good at making friends.

What do you call a ghost that picks on other ghosts?
A boo-lly.

What do you call a man who wears two coats and stands singing in the cemetary?
Max Bygraves.

What do you get if you pour boiling water down a rabbit hole?
Hot cross bunnies.

Which Egyptian Queen was a vampire?
Cleobatra.

What do you call a cannibal who ate his father's sister?
An aunt-eater.

First cannibal: How much did you pay in the restaurant last night?
Second cannibal: £10 a head.

Why do cannibals eat in motorway cafes so often?
Because they specialize in serving truck drivers.

Why do cannibals enjoy weddings so much?
They love toasting the bride and groom.

First cannibal: I don't know what to make of children nowadays.
Second cannibal: How about hotpot.

What's a cannibal's favourite cook book?
'100 Ways to Serve Your Fellow Man'.

How could you help a starving cannibal?
Give him a hand.

What's a cannibal's favourite game?
Swallow My Leader.

Dan: We're having my grandmother for Christmas this year.
Stan: We'll make do with a turkey.

What's the difference between a ghost and a butcher?
One stays awake and the other weighs a steak.

Where do monsters study?
At ghoullege.

What did the ghost sentry say when he heard someone approaching?
"Who ghosts there?"

What could you get if you crossed a snowball with a werewolf?
Frost bite.

Who did the ghost invite to his party?
Anyone he could dig up.

Why do ghosts like tall buildings?
Because they have lots of scarecases.

Which kind of ghost plays cards?
A pokergeist.

What is a ghost's favourite Lake?
Lake Eerie.

If you were surrounded by a ghost, a werewolf, a mummy, Frankenstein's monster, and Dracula, where would you hope to be?
At a fancy dress party.

Ten cats were on a boat and one jumped off. How many were left?
None, they were all copycats.

What happened when the mouse swallowed it's owner's purse by accident?
There was money in the kitty.

Why are cats such popular pets?
Because they're so purr-fect.

What do you give a dog with a fever?
Mustard – it's the best thing for a hot dog.

Where do moggies go on holiday?
Cat-mandu.

What's a cat's favourite TV programme?
The Nine O'clock Mews.

Where do you find a dog with no legs?
Right where you left him.

What did the three-legged cat say when it walked into a Wild West saloon?
"I'm lookin' for a paw."

Which kind of cat cuts grass?
A lawn meower.

What do you call a cat that hangs around in gangs?
A posse.

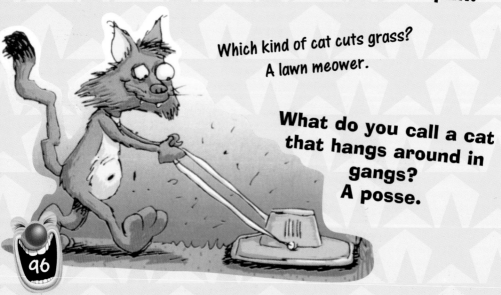

**Which dog keeps the best time?
A watch dog.**

What do you get if you cross a tractor with a dog?
A land-rover.

**Which kind of cereal do cats eat?
Mice crispies.**

When is the vet busiest?
When it's raining cats and dogs.

**What do you call a dog that gets mail?
A golden receiver.**

What is a dog's favourite snack?
Pupcorn.

Have you heard the story about the cat on the roof?
Don't worry about it, it's over your head.

**What does a cat eat when it's hot?
Mice cream.**

PUP CORN

Did you hear about the stupid cowboy who said his horse had six legs? It had forelegs at the front, and two at the back.

Why do cowboys have such fun? Because they're always horsing around.

What did Tonto do when he wanted a mortgage to buy a new house. He went to see the Lone Arranger.

What Native American tribe had most lawyers? The Sioux.

Why did cowboys want to die with their boots on? So they didn't stub their toes when they kicked the bucket.

What did the cowboy say when his dog was run down by a wagon train? "Dawg gone!"

Where do cowboys keep their drinking water? In their ten-gallon hats.

A city man was surprised to see a cowboy walking in town one day, complete with stetson and spurs.

"Excuse me," said the city man. "Are you a real cowboy?"

"Yes," said the cowboy, "and my name's Tex."

"Are you from Texas?" asked the man.

"No," replied the cowboy. "I'm from Louisiana."

What's the difference between a coyote and a flea? One howls on the prairie, the other prowls on the hairy.

"Louisiana? But why are you called Tex?"

"Well, would you want to be called Louise?"

Why did the hedgehog wear spikes to the fancy dress party?
Because it was a sharp dresser.

Why did the football manager flood the pitch?
So he could bring on the sub.

Why did the schoolboy sleep with a banana skin under his pillow?
So he could slip out of bed in the morning.

Why did the archeologist go bankrupt?
Because his career was in ruins.

What did the burglar say to the watchmaker as he tied him up?
"Sorry to take so much of your valuable time."

Why did the policeman hit the clock?
Self-defence! The clock struck twelve.

Why can't you fool a snake?
Because it hasn't got any legs to pull.

Who was the most famous scientist ant?
Albert Anstein.

99

What did the idiot do when he was told he had a flea in his ear? He shot it.

Did you hear about the idiot who changed his mind? The new one didn't work either.

How did the idiot break his leg? He fell into the sink when he was practising tap dancing.

Did you hear about the idiot who phoned his teacher to tell her he couldn't come to school one day because he had lost his voice?

How many idiots does it take to change a lightbulb? Five – one to hold the bulb and four to turn the ladder.

Did you hear about the idiot who made his chickens drink boiling water? He thought they would lay hard boiled eggs.

When an idiot went for a job as a refuse collector, the inspector asked him if he had any experience. "No, sir" replied the idiot. "I thought I'd pick it up as I went along."

What did the idiot do when he found out his room was bugged? He sprayed it with insecticide.

What do you call a monster with sausages on its head?
A head banger.

What do you call a man who lives on the floor?
Matt.

Joe: My wife's gone to the West Indies for a holiday.
Fred: Jamaica?
Joe: No. She wanted to go.

What do you call a man who has fallen into the sea but can't swim?
Bob.

Guest: How much is bed and breakfast?
Manager: £50 a night, sir.
Guest: How much if I make my own bed?
Manager: £30 a night, sir.
Guest: That'll do.
Manager: I'll just get some wood, a hammer and nails then, sir.
Guest: What for?
Manager: I thought you said you wanted to make your own bed?

Have you heard the one about the dead ice cream man? He was found dead in his van, covered in chocolate sauce, whipped cream, and hundreds and thousands. Turns out he'd topped himself.

What do you call a man who is black and blue all over?
Bruce.

What do you call a man with leaves in his trousers?
Russell.

New neighbour: And what might your name be, little boy?
Boy: Well it might be Barnaby, but it's not. It's Charlie.

Guest at posh hotel: This room's okay, but I'd rather have one with a bath.
Porter: You're standing in the lift, sir.

What do you call a soccer fan who is always in tears?
A foot-bawler.

Who growled when he played tennis?
John McEnrover.

Did you hear about the slow swimmer who could only crawl?

Golfer: I love this game. I could go on playing this forever.
Coach: Goodness! Don't you want to improve?

Why do boys play so much football?
They're in it for the kicks.

What's the quietest sport?
Bowling, because you can hear a pin drop.

John: My brother is so thick, he thinks a football coach has four wheels.
Jim: Why? How many does it have?

Why did the yachtsman grab a sack of raisins before he abandoned his sinking boat?
He hoped the currants would carry him safely to shore.

What do you call a girl who lies across the middle of a tennis court?
Annette.

When do swimming trunks go ding dong?
When you wring them out.

102

Why did the stupid pianist keep banging his head against the piano?
He was trying to play by ear.

Why did the composer take twenty baths a day?
He was writing a soap opera.

Did you hear about the composer who spent all day in bed?
He was writing sheet music.

Why did the singer go to the dentist?
To get falsetto teeth.

Teacher: Why do you play that particular piece of music over and over again?
Pupil: Because it haunts me.
Teacher: I'm not surprised. You murdered if the first time you played it.

Who was the vegetarian's favourite pop singer?
Elvis Parsley.

Matt: What's that book the orchestra keeps looking at?
Adil: That's the score.
Matt: Who's winning?

What's a composer's favourite game?
Haydn seek.

Did you hear about the man with the musical moustache?
He was always fiddling with his whiskers.

Why did they arrest the musician?
Because he got into treble.

An old fly and a young fly settled on a man's bald head. The old fly sighed, turned to the young fly and said, "When I was your age, this was only a footpath!"

Sue: Two hippos jumped off a cliff! SPLASH! SPLASH!
Louise: Don't you mean BOOM! BOOM!
Sue: No, they jumped into a river.

Which is a snake's favourite dance?
Snake, rattle and roll.

How would you describe an angry flea?
Hopping mad.

A parrot can't swallow fish.
No, but a peli-can.

What's got a beak, feathers and very long legs?
A duck on stilts.

First rodent: What is the capital of Holland?
Second rodent: Hamsterdam.

A hungry horse had a sports car. What was it's registration? MTGG.

Who invented the Kangaroo?
A bloke with a tin factory
and loads of garoos.

What does a frog do to music?
Hops to it.

What did the elephant say to the mouse who trod on his toe?
"Pick on someone your own size."

Where are elephants found? They're too large to get lost.

Where does a cow go on holiday? Moo York.

How do you stop a dog smelling?
Put a peg on it's nose.

What's orange, hairy and goes up and down?
An orang-utan in a lift.

Knock, Knock!
Who's there?
Dingo.
Dingo who?
Dingo out in case you called.

Doctor, Doctor,
I keep seeing a spinning fly.

Don't worry it's just a bug that's going around.

Knock! Knock!
Who's there?
Doris Duck.
Knock! Knock!
Who's there?
Doris Duck.
Knock! Knock!
Who's there?
Doris Duck.
(Then silence
for a minute
or two).
Knock! Knock!
Who's there?
Oswald Ostrich.
Makes a change
from that duck.

Said one duck to another:
You're driving me quackers.

Bob: I knew a bird that
laid an egg weighing
5kg. Can you beat that?
Jess: Yes, with a whisk.

What's yellow and good
at maths?
A canary with a calculator.

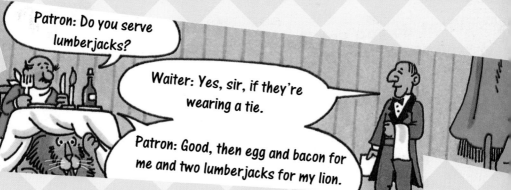

Patron: Do you serve
lumberjacks?

Waiter: Yes, sir, if they're
wearing a tie.

Patron: Good, then egg and bacon for
me and two lumberjacks for my lion.

Why do cows huddle together?   To keep each udder warm.

A man walks into the doctor's surgery. He has a cucumber up his nose, a carrot in his left ear and a banana in his right ear. "What's the matter with me?" he asked. "You're not eating properly," the doctor replied.

What can a whole orange do that half an orange can never do? Look around.

Which room can you never enter? A mushroom.

Why was the mushroom always invited to parties? Because he was a fun guy to have around!

Why did the man drag the cabbage on a lead? He thought it was a collie.

The tomato family were walking home. The son was walking slowly behind, so his dad yelled to him, "Ketchup, son!"

What do you get if you cross a strawberry with a road? A traffic jam.

Why did the orange stop in the middle of the road? Because it ran out of juice.

What's purple, 10,000km long and 12m high? The Grape Wall of China.

What is orange and keeps falling off walls? Humpty Pumpkin.

What did the banana do when the monkey chased it? The banana split.

What do you call two rows of cabbages on the road?
A dual cabbageway.

Fred: Did you ever see a salad bowl?
George: No, but I once saw a horse box.

How do you know carrots are good for your eyes?
Because you never see rabbits wearing glasses.

Why did the apple go out with a fig?
Because it couldn't find a date.

What's round, white and giggles?
A tickled onion.

How can you tell if a calendar is popular?
It has a lot of dates.

What's lemonade?
When you help an old lemon across the road.

Which vegetable needs a plumber?
A leek.

What kind of key opens a banana?
A monkey.

What's a good way of making friends with a werewolf?
Buy him a nice juicy bone.

Which rooms do skeletons not like?
Living rooms.

The Lady Ghost by Sheila Peer

What do monsters sing at Christmas?
'Deck the halls with poison ivy...'

Where do monsters travel?
From ghost to ghost.

Why is Frankenstein never lonely?
He's good at making friends.

Son: Mum, I don't want to go to school. All the children say I look like a werewolf.
Mum: Shut up and comb your face.

What do clocks say on Hallowe'en?
"Tick or treat."

What do you call something with two noses, three mouths, eight ears and red teeth?
Ugly.

On which day do monsters eat people?
Chewsday.

110

What do you get if you cross a witch with an ice cube?
A cold spell.

What do British monsters like to eat?
Fish and ships!

What do you get if a huge, hairy monster steps on Batman and Robin?
Flatman and Ribbon.

Did you see the film about the Abominable Snowman?
It left me cold.

What is big and hairy and bounces up and down?
A monster on a pogo stick.

Where can a monster always find a friend?
In a dictionary.

Why do werewolves do well at school?
Because they're always ready with a snappy answer.

Why was the deadly poisonous snakeman worried?
He'd just bitten his lip.

Where do ghosts go to on the day before a Hallowe'en party?
To the boo-ty parlour.

What do you call a one-eyed monster on a bike?
A Cycle-ops.

Why do demons get on so well with ghouls?
Because demons are a ghoul's best friend.

What do you get if you cross the letter 'T' with an old hag? A t-witch.

What do you get if you cross a mummy with a vampire?
A blood-sucking bandage.

What do you get if you cross a giant monkey with egg-whites and sugar?
A meringue-utan!

What do monsters have for lunch? Human beings on toast.

Why is Duck Beast not welcome in restaurants?
He never settles his bill.

What do you get if you cross a watchdog with a werewolf?
A very nervous postman.

What's crunchy and furry and makes a noise when you pour milk on it? Mice Crispies.

What do you get if you cross a bullfrog with King Kong?
An enormous creature that hops on the Empire State Building and catches aircraft with its tongue.

How many monsters can you fit into an empty car? None...have you ever tried to fit a monster into an empty car?

What do you give to a seasick five-stomached monster? As much room as you can.

What has webbed feet and fangs? Count Quackula.

Which football team do sea monsters support? Slitherpool.

What do you call a monster underneath a car? Jack.

What did the man say when he was told he would be put on the torture rack? "Looks like I'm in for a long stretch."

How many legs can a monster fit into an empty sack? One...the sack isn't empty after that.

The Beast with Talons by Claud Body

What's the best thing to do if five horrible ghosts come in through the front door? Go out through the back door.

What do whales eat?
Fish and ships.

If you drop a white hat into the Red Sea, what does it become?
Wet.

Why did the fish cross the sea?
To get to the other tide.

Which fish are always sleeping?
Kippers.

Which fish only swims at night?
A star fish.

What part of a fish weighs the most?
The scales.

Why did the crab get arrested?
He was always pinching things.

Why did the fish cross the river?
To get to its school.

What do mermaids have on their toast?
Mermerlaid.

How do electric eels
taste?
Shocking.

How did Noah build the ark?
He studied ark-eology.

Which fish
never swim?
Dead fish.

How do you
stop a fish
from smelling?
Cut its nose off.

Why do fish live in
saltwater?
Because pepper
makes them sneeze.

Which fish go to
heaven?
Angel fish.

Where do fish wash?
In a river basin.

What do deaf
fish use?
Herring aids.

What do you get if you cross a clown with a goat? A silly billy.

What keeps sheep warm in winter? Central bleating.

Did you hear the one about the farmer? He was outstanding in his field.

What game do cows play at parties? Moosical chairs.

What do you get if you cross a karate expert with a pig? Pork chops.

Where do sheep go on holiday? The Baahamas.

What do you get if you cross a dinosaur with a pig? Jurassic pork.

What happened when the cow tried to jump over the fence? It was an udder catastrophe.

HONK!

Why did the ram run over the cliff? He didn't see the ewe turn.

Why do cows wear bells? Because their horns don't work.

What did the farmer call the cow that would not give him any milk? An udder failure.

What kind of ties do pigs wear? Pigsties.

What do you get if you sit under a cow? A pat on the head.

Where do cows dance? At the meatball.

What do you call a man with cow droppings all over his shoes? An in cow poop.

What do you call a sleeping cow? A bulldozer.

A lazy young chappie named Ed,
Decided that he'd stay in bed,
"To lie in one place,
In this warm, cosy space,
Is really much better," he said.

Said the doctor, "I think you look ill,
So I'd like you to swallow this pill,
If you're not feeling right,
In another fortnight,
Come back and I'll draw up your will.

There was a professor from Staines,
Whose specialist subject was drains,
He had a collection,
A dredged up selection
Of horrid and gruesome remains.

An especially adventurous bee,
Decided to swim in the sea,
He returned to the hive,
Much more dead than alive,
Having swallowed salt water, you see.

There once was a weedy boy, Tim,
Who went to work out in the gym,
He tripped through the door,
Banged his head on the floor,
And that was the finish of him.

There once was a toad from Kirklees,
That was fond of greenfly and peas,
He went for a beer,
With a mole who lived near,
And was known for his 'Beetles-In-Cheese'.

A crocodile, named Keith,
Once lived in pond near Leith,
He would eat people whole,
Then use a large pole
To scrape the bits out of his teeth.

When bathing young Bertram the bear,
It's best to use waterproof wear,
He makes soggy growls,
And chews up the towels,
While cascades just fly through the air.

There once was a girl named Gayle
Who liked to collect fish in a pail,
But they soon disappeared,
For just as she feared,
They were all eaten up by the whale.

There was a young lady named Trish,
Who never ate aught but raw fish,
She lived near the rocks,
Not far from the docks,
With a tail she couldn't half swish.

What do you call a woman who balances glasses of lager on her nose?

Beatrix.

There's a man at the door with a moustache.
Tell him I've already got one.

What do you call a man who comes through your letterbox?
Bill.

There's a man at the door with a wooden leg.
Tell him to hop it.

There's a man at the door selling beehives.
Tell him to buzz off.

There's a man at the door collecting for the new school swimming pool.
Give him a glass of water.

What do you call a man who's been buried in a bog for twenty years?
Pete.

What do you call a Scottish dinner monitor?
Dinner Ken.

There's a man at the door with an old pram.
Tell him to push off.

There's a man at the door collecting for the old people's home. Shall I give him Grandpa?

There's a man at the door with a bill.
It's probably a duck.

Two men were talking. "Tell me, why is it that when a slice of buttered bread falls to the ground, it always falls buttered side down?" said one. The other man tried to prove him wrong. He buttered a slice of bread and dropped it. "There you are!" he cried, as the bread fell buttered side up. "Ha!" laughed the first man. "You think you're smart! You buttered the bread on the wrong side!"

What do witches ask for in hotels?
Broom service.

What do you call a fly with no wings?
A walk.

Which streets do ghosts haunt?
Dead ends.

Did you hear about the angry flea?
He was hopping mad.

What do you call a fairy that doesn't take baths?
Stinkerbell.

Which exams do young witches have to pass?
Spell-ing tests.

Why did the boy throw butter out of the window?
Because he wanted to see a butter-fly.

What do you say to a skeleton going on holiday?
Bone Voyage.

Have you heard the joke about the butter?
I'd better not tell you, it might spread.

Stan: In China I saw a woman hanging from a tree?
Dave: Shanghai?
Stan: No, just a few feet from the ground.

Bill: My wife and I had a great holiday at the beach this year. We took it in turns to bury each other in the sand.
Ben: Sounds like fun.
Bill: Yes it was – next year I'll go back and dig her up.

"I've never flown before," said the nervous old lady to the air hostess.
"Your pilot will bring me down safely, won't he?"
"Of course, Madam – he's never left anybody up there yet."

What did the great explorer eat in the jungle?
Snake and pygmy pie.

What will they do when the Forth bridge collapses?
Build a fifth bridge.

Dan: A friend of mine decided to travel to Paris by train because of his fear of flying. But he was out of luck.
Stan: Why, what happened?
Dan: His train crashed. A plane fell on it.

Dan: I once travelled all the way from London to Brighton and it didn't cost me a penny.
Stan: How did you manage that?
Dan: I walked.

The trainee pilot was in trouble. He radioed for help.
"Mayday! Mayday!" he gasped. "My engines are on fire!"
The voice from the control tower was calm and business-like.
"Please state your height and position."
"I'm five foot ten and I'm sitting in the cockpit – now please
send help."

I'm terribly sorry for hitting your dog - of course
I'll replace him.

Thank you. How good
are you at
catching rats?

How do you make a Maltese cross?
Tread on his toes.

How do you make a
Swiss roll?
Push him down the hill.

Who succeeded the first
President of the USA?
The second one.

How do you make a
Venetian blind?
Rub soap in his eyes.

Dan and Stan were driving
through London. Stan was
getting worried about his
friend's driving.
"Dan," he asked, "Why do you
always close your eyes
whenever there's a red light?"
"Well," said Dan, "when you've
seen one, you've seen them all!"

Where do you always need an overcoat?
Chile.

How do people eat
cheese in Wales?
Caerphilly.

Why is Europe like a frying pan?
Because it has Greece
at the bottom.

I flew to Paris
last year.

So did I, doesn't it
make your arms
tired though?

123

What cake flies through the air and comes back again?
A boomeringue.

What's the definition of brain food?
Noodle soup.

What is yellow and a whizz at maths?
A banana with a pocket calculator.

What has brown spots and flies?
A school rock bun.

What is pink and wobbly and flies?
A jellycopter.

How can you make an apple puff?
Chase it round the garden a few times.

A rabbit raced a tortoise!
You know the tortoise won.
And Mr Rabbit came in late
A little hot cross bun.

Why did the strawberries cry?
Because they were in a jam.

Waiter! Waiter! This coffee is disgusting.
I wouldn't complain too much sir. You'll be old and weak yourself one day.

How do jellies start their races?
Get set.

Waiter! Waiter! Why does this fish taste of dog food?
Because it's a Rover sole, Sir.

Waiter! Waiter! You've got your sleeve in my soup.
There's no 'arm in that, sir!

124

Waiter! Waiter! It's been an hour since I ordered turtle soup.

What did the spaghetti say to the bolognese?
That's enough of your sauce.

Waiter! Waiter! what is that fly doing on my sorbet?
Learning to ski, sir.

Waiter! Waiter! this lemonade is cloudy.
No sir, it's the glass that's dirty.

What do you call a chip pan that goes into orbit round the earth?
An unidentified frying object.

Who invented pasta?
Someone who knew how to use his noodle.

Waiter! Waiter! I'd like a glass of water and piece of fish, please.
Fillet, Sir?
Right to the top, if you will.

When is roast beef highest in price?
When it's rarest.

What do you call a fake spaghetti?
Mockoroni.

Why did the crab live all alone?
Because he was a hermit.

Doctor, Doctor, I feel like a duck-doo.

What's a duck-doo?

Goes Quack, Quack, of course.

What travels underground at 100mph? A jet-propelled mole.

A man walked into a hotel carrying a pet skunk. "I'd like a double room, please," he said. The receptionist took one look at the skunk and held his nose. "But what about the smell?" "Oh, the skunk doesn't mind at all!" replied the man.

What happened to the stupid water polo player? His horse drowned.

What is juicy, has prickles and four legs? A porcupineapple.

What animal sleeps standing on its head? Yoga bear.

Did you hear about the cat who bought some bandages? It wanted to be a first aid kit.

What is a "butter mountain"?
Two goats riding piggyback on an elephant.

What's the best way to cut through giant waves?
Use a sea saw.

First Snake: I'm having a party. Will you blow up all the balloons?
Second Snake: Why ask me?
First Snake: Because you're a puff adder.

Why do elephants make good musicians? Because they're great trumpters.

What wallows in mud and squeaks?
A hippopotamouse.

Which animal works very hard?
A beaver.

Which food swings through trees?
Monkey nuts.

What do you call a hippo that is feeling very pleased with itself?
A happypotamus.

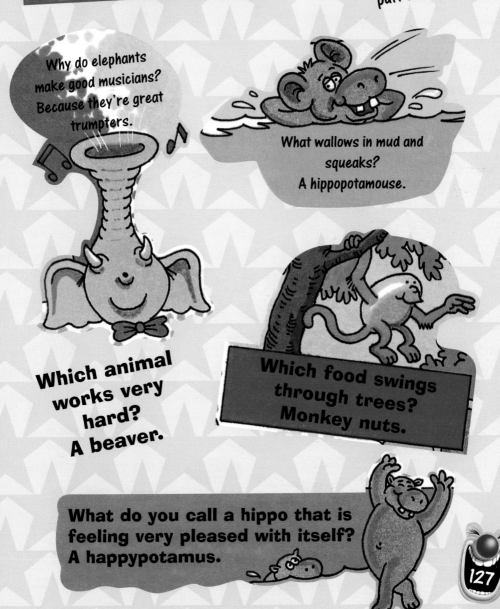

What do you call a nervous elephant? A jellyphant.

What ape works as a chef at the burger bar? A grilla.

Who wrote the book: My life with the Herd? L. E. Phant.

What do you do if you find an elephant in your hammock? Sling it somewhere else.

What do you get if you cross a sheep with a rainstorm? A wet blanket.

What do you call a grasshopper with no legs? A grasshover.

What's orange, hairy and keeps returning? A boomerang-utan.

What do you get if you cross an elephant and a kangaroo? Big potholes all over the outback.

What do you call a herd of elephants in a water-hole?
Swimming trunks.

What goes swim, purr, swim, meow?
A catfish.

Why did the crayfish blush?
Because it saw the ship's bottom.

What goes up slowly and comes down quickly?
An elephant in a lift.

What roars and swims underwater?
A sea lion.

What do you call an elephant between two bits of toast?
A jumbo sandwich.

What goes now you see me, now you don't?
A penguin on a zebra crossing.

Who lives in the desert and writes plays?
Sheik Speare.

A conjurer who was entertaining on a cruise-liner always employed a chatty talking parrot in his act. Polly would make the odd amusing remark. "This evening, I shall perform a most unusual illusion," announced the conjurer.

At that moment, the ship's boiler blew up, after which the parrot was next seen floating by on a piece of wreckage in the sea. The dazed conjurer was clinging on wearily beside him, while the parrot squawked, "I've seen some stupid tricks in my time, but..."

Three pieces of string went to a restaurant for supper. The first piece of string walked in and the waiter asked, "Are you a string?" "Yes," the string replied, so the waiter said, "I'm sorry, we don't serve pieces of string." Undeterred, the second string tried to get a table, but the waiter refused to serve him saying, "I'm sorry, we just don't serve string." So the third string tied himself in a knot and frayed the end. He walked into the restaurant and when the waiter asked, "Are you a string?" he calmly replied, "No, I'm a frayed knot."

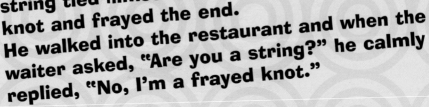

It was very hot on the African plain, but a lion was keeping cool thanks to a herd of elephants, who were flapping their huge ears all around him. When a hot leopard arrived, he asked the elephants to keep him cool too, but they refused.

"How come they won't flap their ears for me, but they will for you?" the leopard asked the lion.

"Simple," replied the lion. "They're my fan club."

"I'm worried about my pet chimpanzee," its owner told the vet. "It keeps banging itself on the head with a clenched fist."

"Leave him with me," replied the vet. "Come back for him in a few days."

So the owner went away feeling very relieved. When he returned, he was delighted to find that the chimpanzee was cured.

"How did you manage it?" the owner asked the vet.

"Simple," replied the vet. "I gave the chimp a big mallet. He hit himself so hard that he lost his memory and quite forgot ever to do it again!"

How did Frankenstein's monster eat its food? It bolted it down.

What did the Three Wise Men bring the baby monster? Gold, Frankenstein and Myrrh.

Who's the most famous ghost in politics? The Spooker of the House of Commons.

Where do ghosts send their laundry? To the dry screamers.

Who wrote a biography of Frankenstein's monster? Tess Tube.

What did the first hippy ghost say to the second hippy ghost? Ghoul, man, ghoul.

How does a ghost look when it's worried? Very grave.

What kind of books does Frankenstein's monster like best? Anything with a good cemetery plot.

What is an executioner's favourite meal?
He likes a good chop.

Doctor, Doctor, every night when I go to sleep I have horrible nightmares. I think there are giant monsters waiting under my bed. What can I do?
Doctor: Saw the legs off your bed.

What can happen to people who study Egyptian mummies?
They can get wrapped up in their work!

Why was the ghost rushed to hospital? To have his ghoul stones removed.

Why don't witches like to ride their brooms when they're angry? They're afraid of flying off the handle.

They're going to make a film about the Loch Ness Monster and a shark from Jaws. It will be called 'Loch Jaws'!

Two phantoms were playing a game of table tennis. One was losing so badly that he didn't have a ghost of a chance of winning!

What would you see at a chicken show?
Hentertainment.

What do you get if you cross a rooster with a bell?
An alarm cluck.

What did the chicken say to the farmer?
Nothing – chickens can't talk.

AAAK!

Why did the chicken cross the road and roll in the dirt, then cross the road again?
Because he was a dirty double-crosser.

What do you call a chicken in a shellsuit?
An egg.

Why did the turkey cross the road?
To prove that he wasn't a chicken.

What kind of book tells you all about chickens?
A hencyclopedia.

What do you get if you cross a cow, a sheep and a goat?
The milky baa kid.

Why did the chewing gum cross the road?
Because it was stuck to the chicken's foot.

What do sheep call their best friends?
Pen pals.

What do you get if you cross a young sheep and a penguin?
A lamb's-wool dinner jacket.

What do lady sheep call their coats?
Ewe-niforms.

Where do sheep go on holiday?
Ramsgate.

Doctor! Doctor! I've just swallowed a sheep!
How do you feel?
Very Baa-a-d.

What do you call a sheep without legs?
A cloud.

A man walked into a butcher's shop and asked the butcher if he had a sheep's head.
"No," said the butcher. "It's just the way I part my hair."

What would you get if you crossed a penguin, a sheep and a kangaroo?
A black and white woolly jumper.

Big Ugg was the first to make fire;
He stared at it, full of desire.
Then he lost self-control,
And he swallowed it whole,
And it didn't half make him perspire.

Ballooning's an interesting antic –
Serene and relaxing, not frantic;
Unless a typhoon
Spoils your quiet afternoon,
And deposits you in the Atlantic.

The caves in the
Stone Age were dusty,
And chilly, and
draughty, and musty;
But surely much worse
Was the terrible curse
Of the Iron Age, with
everything rusty.

So sad is what happened to Jake,
Who stood on a worm by mistake.
He very soon found
That the 'worm' on the ground
Was the end of a whopping great snake.

BUZZ, BUZZ

Said a fellow (much dafter than me!),
"All day long I shall mimic a bee."
But although he spent hours
Buzz-buzzing round flowers,
He couldn't make honey for tea.

BUZZ

TWIT

136

When counting his family, Mark Evans,
Said, "There's triplets, and quads, oh! Good heavens.
I've also twin daughters
At three and three-quarters,
And my sons are at sixes and sevens."

A saucy young spider named Megs,
Was proud of her eight hairy legs.
"Though I've only got two,"
Said her chicken friend Prue,
"I can cackle, and fly, and lay eggs."

When nimble young Nicola Knox
Was climbing about on the rocks,
Warned her friend, "If you choose
To take off your shoes,
You'll get great big holes in your socks."

Jim's crowing made neighbours so sore,
That they banged on his chicken-house door.
He exclaimed, "Don't they know
That a cockerel must crow?
To annoy them, I'll crow even more."

Now Freddie the flea was a whopper,
A truly magnificent hopper.
But when mixing a vault
With a back somersault,
That's when he came a real cropper.

Mr and Mrs Brown were arriving in the airport, ready to take off for their holiday in Greece.
"I wish I'd brought the piano," said Mr Brown suddenly.
"Whatever for?"
"I left our tickets on it."

Tourist: How do I get to the London Palladium?
Musician: Practice.

Have you missed your train, sir?

Of course not. I didn't like the look of it, so I chased it out of the station.

Where do Londoners with pimples live?
Ackney.

The French hitch-hiker was thrilled when the English car drew up alongside him.
"Want a lift, mate?" asked the driver.
"Oui, oui!" said the hitch-hiker excitedly.
"Not in my car you don't!" said the driver.

Fred: Cabby – how much will it cost to take me to the station?
Taxi driver: A fiver.
Fred: How much for my suitcase?
Taxi driver: No charge.
Fred: OK then – you take my suitcase to the station, and I'll walk.

Waiter on the cruise ship: Here's your lunch, Sir.

UGG!

Passenger: Just throw it over the side and save me the trouble.

She stood on the bridge at midnight,
Her lips all a-quiver.
She gave a cough; her leg fell off
And floated down the river.

Hickory Dickory Dock,
Two mice ran up the clock.
The clock struck one
But the other escaped with only
minor injuries.

Harry: My Dad's teaching me to be a Channel swimmer. Every day he takes me a little bit further out to sea and I have to swim back to shore.
Garry: That's great, don't you find it hard, though?
Harry: The swimming bit's fine – the hard bit is getting out of the sack!

Young Thomas
invited disaster
By running downstairs
ever faster.
He tripped and he fell
With a shriek and a yell.
Now he's totally covered
in plaster.

Polly: My boyfriend reminds me of the sea.
Dolly: You mean he's wild, restless and romantic?
Polly: No – he makes me sick.

Harry: When the headmaster retired from our school the pupils gave him an illuminated address.
Garry: How lovely. How did they manage that?
Harry: They burned his house down.

A man went into a hardware shop and asked for rat poison.
"Sorry," said the assistant, "We don't stock it – have you tried Boots?"
"For heaven's sake, I want to poison them, not kick them to death!"

"Dad, dad, I've just seen a cow fall down!" said a little boy anxiously.
"Don't get upset," replied his father. "It's no good crying over spilt milk!"

What do you call elephants without trunks? Nudists.

Why did the cockerel laugh at the chicken? Because it told a cracking yolk.

Who wrote the book, 'All About Dogs'? Al Satian.

Which horses have the shortest ears? The smallest ones.

Why did the elephant put corn in his shoes? Because he was pigeon-toed.

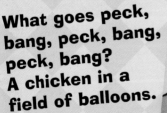

What goes peck, bang, peck, bang, peck, bang? A chicken in a field of balloons.

What's the hardest thing about learning to ride a horse? The ground.

What goes pitter-patter ninety-eight times, then CLOP, CLOP?
A centipede wearing a pair of clogs.

An elephant went for a walk,
He came across a skunk,
Then turned and ran the other way,
He wished he had no trunk!

Doctor, Doctor, I keep thinking I'm a parrot.
Well, perch yourself over there and I'll see you in a moment.

Doctor, Doctor, I keep thinking I'm a cat.

Take this medicine and you'll be purrrrfectly alright.

What didn't the father cow want to play games with the baby cow?
Because he wasn't in the moood!

Did you hear about the hunter who disappeared?
Apparently, something he disagreed with, ate him!

What purrs and performs gymnastic feats?
An acrocat.

What do you call a cow that lives in Greenland?
An Eskimoo.

Knock Knock
Who's there?
A shoe.
A shoe who?
Bless you.

Knock Knock
Who's there?
Avenue.
Avenue who?
Avenue heard this joke before?

**Knock Knock
Who's there?
Radio.
Radio who?
Radio not, here I come.**

**Knock Knock
Who's there?
Max.
Max who?
Max no difference, just open
the door.**

Knock Knock
Who's there?
Norma Lee.
Norma Lee who?
Norma Lee I'd use the
bell, but it's broken so I
had to knock.

**Knock Knock
Who's there?
Police.
Police who?
Police stop telling me these
stupid jokes!**

Knock Knock
Who's there?
Winner.
Winner who?
Winner you going to
get this doorbell
fixed?

Knock Knock
Who's there?
Alex.
Alex who?
Alex plain later, let me in.

*Knock Knock
Who's there?
Weirdo.
Weirdo who?
Weirdo you think
you're going?*

**Knock Knock
Who's there?
Dishes.
Dishes who?
Dishes the police –
open up!**

Patient: Well, Doctor, how do I stand.
Doctor: I've no idea, it's a miracle.

Doctor, Doctor, my boy is so tall. He seems to have grown another foot this year.
Well, I would enter him in a three-legged race.

Patient: Can you give me something for wind.
Doctor: Yes, take this kite.

Doctor, Doctor, I feel like I want to paint everything in gold.
You've got a gilt complex.

Doctor, I feel like a goat.
Well, how are the kids?

Doctor, I think there's something wrong with my stomach.
Well, keep your coat buttoned up and no-one will notice.

143

What has a
very long neck
and floats?
A giraft.

What wears a cloak, visits granny in the woods
and goes, "Oink, oink!"?
Little Red Riding Hog!

What roars and can be
found in a flower bed?
A snapdragon.

Did you hear about the
kangaroo who married a
polar bear?
Yes, they had a little
polar-necked jumper.

Knock, Knock!
Who's there?
Cook!
Cook Who?
It must be spring.

What carried passengers and has lots of humps?
A camel train.

Have you ever seen a pie that flies?
Yes, a magpie.

Knock, Knock!
Who's there?
Noah!
Noah who?
Noah place where I
can live?

What tree gallops?
A horse chestnut.

Why did Miss Muffet run
away from the creepy crawly?
Because 's spied 'er!

144

First dog: Just listen to those cats howling!

Second dog: It may sound awful to us, but it's mewsic to their ears!

What do you call a cow with no legs? Ground beef.

The grape was all a-flutter,
Then it began to pine,
For a herd of elephants squashed it,
And now the grape is wine.

What do you get if you cross a spring bulb and a croc? A daffodile.

What do you call a musical dog? The hound of music.

First Swan: Last Saturday, all the birds from our local pond played the river birds at cricket, and would you believe, our captain was bowled first ball!

Second Swan: Really, you mean he was out for a duck.

Who writes jokes about spooks?
A ghost writer.

What did the mother ghost say to the baby ghost?
Put your boos and shocks on.

Where do ghosts get their jokes?
They have a crypt writer.

What's a cold, evil candle called?
The wicked wick of the north.

What happens when you fail to pay your exorcist?
You get repossessed.

Why did the ghost go in the elevator?
To raise his spirits.

Why are skeletons usually so calm?
Nothing gets under their skin.

What happens when a ghost gets lost in the fog?
He is mist.

What is a ghost's favourite salad dressing?
Boo-cheese dressing.

Why did the skeleton give up his job? Because his heart wasn't in it.

What did the first ghost magician say to the second ghost magician? I can see right through your tricks.

What's a ghost's favourite food? Ghoul-ash.

How can you tell if a school is haunted? It has school spirit.

Why did the skeleton run from the battle? Because he didn't have the guts for a fight.

What do you call a skeleton that won't get out of bed? Lazy Bones.

What kind of jokes do skeletons laugh at most? Rib-ticklers.

What shellfish do skeletons like most? Muscles.

What day of the week do ghosts like best? Tombsday.

Said Sammy, the sad centipede,
"I've many more legs than I need.
I'd be just as nifty
If I had only fifty,
And what's more, I'd cost less to feed.

Old Pythagoras had a good ruse
For triangle solvers to use.
"Add the squares of each side,"
He explained, with some pride,
"That's the square of the hypotenuse."

An animal lover called Cilla,
Went sailing with her pet gorilla.
They took several knocks,
And landed on rocks,
When he pushed the wrong way on the tiller.

The mathematics teacher told Mabel,
"You simply must learn every table,
You'll then be so quick
at arithmetic,
That to take every prize you'll
be able."

A ghost who was
causing confusion
By his very unwelcome intrusion,
In a family's new home
He mistook for his own,
Said, "Sorry, I'm just an illusion."

A grumpy old blackbird named Shirley,
Complained, "Though I'm always up early,
I can't find any bugs,
Caterpillars or grubs,
And the worms that I catch are too curly."

Said Sue's Mum, "I've made a decision.
You must sit down and do your revision."
"What you want me to do,
Is not fair," replied Sue,
"When I'd much rather watch television."

A careful beekeeper from Sydenham,
Protected his bees with a lid on 'em.
He said, "It's not nice,
If they're eaten by mice,
But I really just cannot get rid of 'em."

A cheerful young glutton named Ben,
Ate some very large meals now and then.
He fastened his lips
Around steak, eggs and chips,
Bacon, sausage and barbecued hen.

When young Jim took a dip in the river,
He said to his friend, with a shiver,
"It has frozen my heart,
And my feet, for a start,
And it gives me a cold in the liver."

First bird: My neighbour was arrested.

Second bird: Why?

First bird: Because he was always Robin.

Two shellfish were chatting, when one suddenly stopped talking. What did the first shellfish say?
Don't clam up on me.

The python's such a friendly snake,
How he likes to hug.
He'll grip you in his mighty coils,
And hold you oh-so-snug!

Doctor, Doctor, I keep thinking I'm a bird. You must stop getting in a flap.

Which cow always keeps warm? A Jersey.

What's huge, slippery and has a trunk? A eelephant.

What did the crab say when offered salt?
Just a pinch.

What did the big buffalo say to the little buffalo? Bye, son.

First cowboy: I call my horse Isaiah.

Second cowboy: Why?

First cowboy: Because one Isaiah than the other.

What do you call an animal with two heads, five legs and a prickly tail?
Ugly.

Who wrote the book, 'Tropical Fish'?
Barry Cuder.

What do you get if you cross a giraffe and a cow?
Very tall milkshakes!

Garry: Do you water a horse when he's thirsty?
Dad: Yes, that's right.
Garry: Then I'm going to the kitchen to milk the cat.

An ostrich saw an egg that a budgie had laid.
"I've never seen an egg that is so small!" he told the budgie.
"I'm not surprised," replied the budgie. "Usually, you've got your head in the sand."

Knock, Knock!
Who's there?
Aunty.
Aunty who?
Aunty Lope!

Where does a sick horse go?
Horspital.

Why did the farmer call his horse Blacksmith?
The horse kept making a bolt for the door!

Two elephants went to a fair. "Let's ride on the merry-go-round!" said the first.

"They make me dizzy!" said the second.

"You go on and I'll watch!"

So the first elephant agreed. But after a moment or two, the merry-go-round went out of control. It spun faster and faster, until the elephant was thrown off.

"Are you hurt?" cried the second elephant, hurrying up.

"Of course I am!" replied the first elephant, rather shaken. "I went round five times and you didn't even wave."

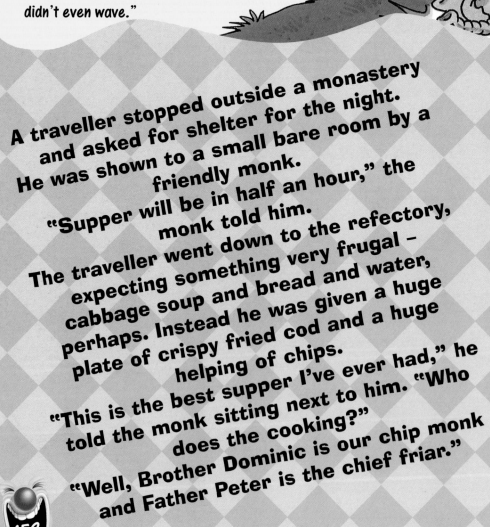

A traveller stopped outside a monastery and asked for shelter for the night. He was shown to a small bare room by a friendly monk.

"Supper will be in half an hour," the monk told him.

The traveller went down to the refectory, expecting something very frugal – cabbage soup and bread and water, perhaps. Instead he was given a huge plate of crispy fried cod and a huge helping of chips.

"This is the best supper I've ever had," he told the monk sitting next to him. "Who does the cooking?"

"Well, Brother Dominic is our chip monk and Father Peter is the chief friar."

A little boy called Simon Mickey Tune came home from his first day at school in a temper.

"What's wrong, Simon?" asked his mother.

"It's my teacher. She won't call me by my proper name. She calls me Simon Tune."

"But most people aren't called by their full names."

"I don't care about most people," said Simon. "I don't like having the Mickey taken out of me."

Three tortoises went into a café and ordered three chocolate milk shakes. Then it started to rain so they decided that one of them should go and fetch an umbrella. The tortoise who offered to go was very worried that the others would drink his milk shake while he was gone. But when they assured him they wouldn't, he finally set off. Two days passed and still he had not returned; then another two days. Finally, after a week, one of the tortoises who was still waiting said, "He definitely won't be coming back now! Let's drink his milk shake."

"I agree!" said the second tortoise. Suddenly the third tortoise shouted angrily from the café doorway, "If you dare touch it, I won't go for the umbrella!"

An elderly lady from Crewe,
Dropped her false teeth down the loo.
She pulled on the chain,
They popped up again,
And bit her, the silly old moo.

A seedy old gardener
called Bertie,
Pinched a young girl who
got shirty,
She picked up the shears
And cut off his ears,
(Which, needless to say,
were quite dirty).

There once was an
old maid from Dunlin,
Who went on a mad highland fling.
Her life which was spartan,
Is now much more tartan,
And everything
goes with
a swing.

A Mexican dancer called Fritz,
Said he could do the splits.
But when he let rip,
He busted his zip,
And shook his maracas to bits.

There was a pop star called Reg Dwight,
Whose trousers were dangerously tight.
When he started to move
They got stuck in the groove,
And now he sings opera all night.

An unhappy young kangaroo,
Said, when in his Australian zoo,
"I just sit here all day,
And they won't let me play,
On my bongos and didgeridoo."

The magician did
tricks so mysterious,
That he drove all his
audience delirious.
But when asked by
friend Dennis,
To make England win tennis,
He said, "Really, you cannot
be serious."

When Gary the gardener
grew peas,
He had this remarkable wheeze.
"If I plant them with ice,
It will be very nice,
They'll grow frozen, so
no need to freeze.

When Caroline's mother made custard,
She started to get a bit flustered.
Her daughter said, "What
You have got is too hot,
Put your specs on, the label says
'mustard'."

Young Jenny was
reading a book,
On how to catch
fish with a hook.
"It's a much
better bet,"
Said her friend,
"with a net.
Then you'll catch
more than you
can cook."

Why did the farmer call his pig 'Ink'?
Because he kept running out of the pen.

Why didn't the pigs listen to their father?
Because he was such a boar.

Townie: What's your pig's name?
Farmer: Ballpoint.
Townie: Is that its real name?
Farmer: No, it's his pen name!

Why are pigs such unappreciative animals?
Because they take their food for grunted.

What's pink, has a curly tail and drinks blood?
A hampire.

What's a pig's favourite ballet?
Swine Lake.

Joe: What do your parents do?
Fred: They raise pigs.
Joe: So that's why you eat like that.

What do you call a stupid pig thief?
A ham burglar.